ROME · FLORENCE

THE VATICAN AND THE SIXTINE CHAPEL

AND SURROUNDINGS

VENICE · NAPLES

MURANO - BURANO

POMPEII - HERCULANEUM - VESUVIUS
CAPRI - ISCHIA - SORRENTO

A WONDERFUL JOURNEY
THROUGH HISTORY AND ART
OF THE FOUR PEARLS OF ITALY

300 COLOUR PHOTOGRAPHS
CITY PLANS

BONECHI

D1405572

© Copyright by CASA EDITRICE BONECHI
Via Cairoli, 18/b Firenze - Italia
Tel. 055/576841 - Fax 055/5000766
E-mail: bonechi@bonechi.it   Internet: www.bonechi.it

Printed in Italy by Centro Stampa Editoriale Bonechi

Texts
Florence and Venice: by the editorial staff of the Publishing House.
Rome: text by Fabio Boldrini, Leonardo Castellucci, Stefano Giuntoli and
by the editorial staff of the Publishing House.
Napoli: by Giuliano Valdes, Editing Studio-Pisa and by the editorial staff
of the Publishing House.

Cover: Manuela Ranfagni

Photographic References
Foto Tripodi: page 188
Lucilla Izzi: pages 161, 168 (bottom), 181, 192 (bottom)
Mario Pirone: page 169
Sergio Riccio: page 178
Ufficio Stampa San Carlo/Foto Luciano Romano: page 170 (bottom)
Photographs from the Archives of Casa Editrice Bonechi taken by:
Gaetano Barone, Carlo Cantini, CISCU Lucca, Gianni Dagli Orti, Foto
aerea I-BUGA, Foto Musei Vaticani, Foto Rev. da Fabbrica di San Pietro in
Vaticano, Paolo Giambone, Stefano Giusti, Italfotogieffe, K&B News,
Antonio Lelli, Maurilio Mazzola, M.S.A., Nicolò Orsi Battaglini, Mario
Pirone, Andrea Pistolesi, Pubbli Aer Foto, Antonio Quattrone, Alessandro
Saragosa, Soprintendenza Archeologica per la Toscana, Soprintendenza ai
Monumenti di Firenze, Fabrizio Tempesti, Mario Tonini.

ISBN 88-476-0037-5

***

Foreword

Rome, Florence, Venice, Naples: four gems of art, but also four cornerstones of history, and not only of Italy but of Western civilization as a whole. As far back as antiquity, fundamental stages in the march of civilisation bear the mark of writers, philosophers, artists, condottieri, travelers born here or for whom one of these cities was of reference.

The small village of the Palatine hill that was Rome went on to conquer the entire Mediterranean basis, crossing the Channel, pushing on to the Red Sea, the Caspian Sea and the Persian Gulf, certainly by force of arms but above all with its culture, the signs of which are much more lasting and can still be encountered in works of art, languages, the legal system. The ships that plied the «Mare Nostrum» as the Romans called the Mediterranean, transported not only multitudes of soldiers but products of all kinds to be sold in the farthest provinces; provinces where the inhabitants could proudly affirm: «Civis romanus sum», .«I am a citizen of Rome». And together with the wine and wheat, off, spices, pottery, raw materials, gold, what travelled on those ships were ideas. Then came centuries of decadence, with the Barbarian invasions and the breaking up of the empire. But not the end. Rome was destined to find a new place for itself in history and art thanks to the Church and the popes who succeeded in infusing new life.

The long period of renewal which began in the fifteenth century enriched Rome with splendid masterworks created by artists who flocked into the city from the various Italian courts. By the sixteenth century Rome had won back its role, albeit on a different level, of «caput mundi» or head of the world thanks to the great artists whose names, and let that of Michelangelo stand for them all, are known throughout the world.

The impression imparted by Rome is that of grandeur, but what strikes the visitor to Florence is its elegance and beauty. While its countless palaces and churches bear witness to an opulent past, it is the essence of things in this city «on a human scale», that counts for more than show. Florence turned to man and he became the city's focal point: man with his intelligence, initiative, creativity, genius.

It was here that the spoken language of the people first achieved standing as literature (and what a formidable work it was!) here that the illustrious artists who created the splendor of Florence were born but they also beautified Rome and enriched all of Italy. It was here that merchants and bankers created immense fortunes and expanded throughout Europe; here that Humanism and the Renaissance, furnishing new impetus to the Letters and the Arts, came into being. It was here that inspired minds were at work, leaving their indelible mark. Yet the emotions aroused in those who visit Florence are more intimate, and perhaps more profound, than elsewhere. What strikes them is the serene and conscious beauty of the monuments, rather than their grandeur. Art is present in the air one breathes and emanates from the cobbles of lane and street as much as it does from the ashlar and marble facing of palace and church. In the countless shops able craftsmen hand on the skill of their illustrious ancestors: nowadays the foreigners too come to Florence «a bottega», as «apprentices» to learn the art of the goldsmith, marquetry, cabinet work, carving.

In its monuments Venice, for centuries queen of the Adriatic and the largest and busiest trading center on the entire Mediterranean thanks to its exchange of goods with the Muslim Near East, reflects its role as a bridge between west and east.

The town originated and developed under the protection of Byzantium, until its power became such that it turned into a dangerous rival. «Fondachi» or warehouses were opened on the shores of the eastern Mediterranean as well as in central Europe, and while its ships plied the seas bearing a wealth of prized wares and fighting Slavic and Saracen pirates, other merchants were travelling the Silk Route through the boundless lands of Asia: Marco Polo with his father and his uncle were received with all honors at the court of the great Kublai Khan who entrusted them with diplomatic missions.

The Serenissima was born from the sea and lives from the sea: its palaces seem to emerge from the water and the streets are canals. Its artistic personality was formed in the seas of the Near East, in Byzantium. The Basilica of St. Mark's is Veneto-Byzantine and the mosaics which glow inside are Byzantine. The flamboyant Gothic of Venice evokes Moorish architecture and its palaces are unmistakable. Wherever they appear, in Dalmatia or in Greece, they are recognizable immediately as Venetian architecture.

The city is unique not only in its history, structure, art, but also in its way of life, with its floating markets, its elegant and typical gondolas which glide silently along the rii; they are more than tourist conveyances for they mark the fundamental stages of life for every Venetian: the nuptial procession moves by gondola.

Parthenope, Palaeopolis, Neapolis, Naples: names which represent the origins and historical transformation of a city through the centuries: from its foundation as a colony of Cumae, an early settlement of Greek seafarers from the city of Kumè in Asia Minor (Magna Graecia), to periods of domination by the Greeks and the Romans, the Swabians, Angevins and Aragonese, and again by the Bourbons; then came the short period of the Parthenopean Republic followed by the influence of the French and the Jacobins, and finally the Unification of Italy, and modern-day Naples which has just recently been undergoing a cultural reawakening. Naples as a capital city: a city subjected to a whole series of dominations, managing nevertheless to hold on to a unique cultural identity which, despite its countless contradictions, has still kept it in the ranks of "capital" city.

This book hopes to be a compendium of the beauties these four cities offer the visitor, a valid tool in helping to appreciate them, a travel companion which will highlight the most characteristic aspects of each one and which will help to keep its memory fresh long after we have moved on to other shores.

ROME

Rome began when groups of shepherds and farmers settled on the hill now known as the Palatine. Etymologically Roma may mean the city of the river, or more probably the city of the Ruma, an old Etruscan family.

After the semi-legendary period of the monarchy, the first authentic historical references date to the moment of transition from the monarchy to the republic (509 B.C.), when the Etruscan civilization, which had dominated Rome with the last kings, began its slow decline. The long period of the republic was marked by the formation of a real democracy governed by the consuls and the tribunes (the former represented the so-called plebeians), which went so far as to institute equal rights for patricians and plebs.

In the 4th century B.C. Rome already held sway over all of Latium and later extended its rule to many other regions in Italy, subjugating numerous Italic peoples and the great Etruscan civilization. Even the Gauls, and the Greeks in southern Italy, laid down their arms to Rome and by 270 B.C. the entire Italian peninsula had fallen under Roman domination. In the 3rd century B.C. this power began to spread out beyond the borders of the peninsula. Between 264 and 201 B.C. the entire Mediterranean (with the Punic wars) fell under Roman rule, and in the east, Rome extended its frontiers into Alexander the Great's kingdom, and in the west, subjugated the Gauls and the peoples of Spain. It is at this point that the republic became an empire, beginning with auspices of power and greatness under Augustus.

The empire, as it was conceived, was meant to be a balanced mixture of the various republican magistratures under the direct control of the senate and the will of the people. This was what it was meant to be, but in reality as time passed the empire took on an ever increasing dictatorial and militaristic aspect. With its far-flung frontiers, Rome found itself divided and split and as its authority began to wane, it went into a slow but inexorable decadence. The city was no longer the emperor's seat and the senate continued to lose its political identity. This decadence reached its zenith after the first barbarian invasions, but the city never lost its moral force, that awareness which for centuries had considered Rome the caput mundi, a situation which was also abetted by the advent of Christianity which consecrated it as the seat of its Church.

After the middle of the 6th century A.D., Rome became just another of the cities of the new Byzantine empire, with its capital in Ravenna. Even so, two centuries later, thanks to the presence of the Pope, it once more became a reference point for this empire and its history becomes inseparable from that of the Franco-Carolingian empire. Charlemagne chose to be crowned emperor in Rome and hereafter all emperors were to be consecrated as such in Rome.

The city proclaimed itself a free commune in 1144. In this period it was governed by the municipal powers, the papacy and the feudal nobility. The powers of the commune and those of the pope were often in open contrast and were marked by harsh struggles. At the beginning of the 14th century the papacy moved to Avignon and the popular forces were freer to govern. At the end of the 14th century and in the early 15th century the situation once more was reversed: the pope returned to Rome and managed to gain control of the city and recuperate most of the power the popular government had gained in the preceding century. The city flourished in this period, for it became the capital of the Papal State and was as splendid as ever, one of the most important crossroads for culture and art. In the centuries that followed, politically Rome tended towards an ever greater isolation: the Papal State kept at a distance from the various international contrasts and while this set limits on its importance from a political point of view it gave free rein to a development of trade and above all the arts and culture.

This situation continued up to the end of the 18th century when the revolutionary clime which struck Europe in those years also involved the Church in an unexpected crisis and the papal rule of the city passed to the Republic (Pius VI was exiled to France). Temporal power had a brief comeback with Pius VII, but only a few years later Napoleon once more revolutionized the situation, proclaiming Rome the second city of his empire. After varying vicissitudes in which the city returned to the pope (1814), came the period of the Risorgimento when, under the papacy of Pius IX, Rome was a ferment of patriotic and anticlerical ideals.

In 1848 a real parliament was formed; the following year the Roman Republic was proclaimed and the government passed into the hands of a triumvirate headed by Giuseppe Mazzini until the intervention of the French army restored temporal power. In 1860 with the formation of the Kingdom of Italy, the pope's power was limited to Latium alone. Ten years later, with the famous episode of the breach at Porta Pia, the French troops protecting the papacy were driven out of the city, which was annexed to the Kingdom of Italy and became its capital. Dissension arose between the Papal State and the new Italian political reality which eventually led to the conciliation between the State and the Church in the Lateran Pact (Feb. 11, 1929). After World War II, when Italy passed from the monarchy to the republic, Rome became the seat of the Italian Parliament.

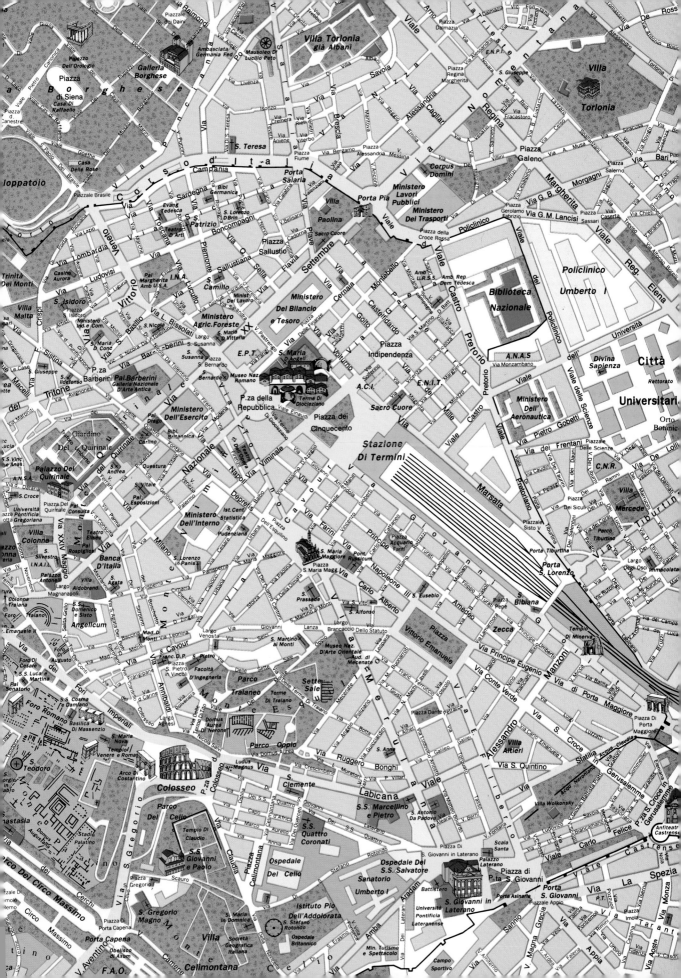

*The staircase of the Capitoline with the statue of the Dioscuri
and the Palazzo Senatorio.*

THE CAPITOLINE

From earliest times on, the Capitoline hill (or Campidoglio) was the center of the political, social, and religious life of Rome. In addition to the old *asylum*, this was the site of the great Italic temple dedicated to the Capitoline Jupiter, and the name of *Capitolium* was used almost exclusively to designate the temple rather than the entire site. Among others the *arx*, with the Temple of Iuno Moneta (the Admonisher) and the temple of the Virtus, also stood on the northern tip of the two knolls which comprised the height. The *clivus capitolinus* was the carriage road which led to the hill of the forum; there was also a flight of stairs which led to the arx alone and from which, near the Mamertine Prisons, the famous *Scalae Gemoniae* branched off.

The most sacred of the hills of Rome (even though the smallest) has continued to be the seat of power throughout the centuries. Michelangelo's **Piazza del Campidoglio** now stands on its summit, defined by illustrious palaces and magnificently decorated by the **statue of Marcus Aurelius**, set at the center of the intriguing interplay of ellipses and volutes Michelangelo himself designed on the gray pavement of the square. Formerly in the Lateran square, the Marcus Aurelius was moved to the Capitoline in 1538 and had not apparently

been previously taken into consideration by Michelangelo as decoration for the square.

The Palazzo Senatorio, the Palazzo Nuovo (or of the Capitoline Museum) and the Palazzo de'Conservatori define the limits of this first plateau of modern Rome. Both the **Palazzo Nuovo** and the **Palazzo dei Conservatori** were designed as twins by Michelangelo and built respectively by Girolamo Rainaldi (under Innocent X) and Giacomo della Porta (after 1563). Both of Michelangelo's palaces are characterized by an architectural layout sustained by large Corinthian pilasters, and are crowned by an attic with a balustrade supporting large statues.

The **Palazzo Senatorio**, however, with a facade that is attributed to Rainaldi and Della Porta (although there was an earlier project by Michelangelo) stands on the historical site of the *Tabularium* and is distinguished by its converging flights of stairs, designed by Michelangelo and built while the artist was still alive. Inside is a series of famous rooms, including the *Sala delle Bandiere*, that of the *Carroccio* (or *Chariot*), the *Green Room*, the *Yellow Room*, and the large *Council Hall* where the Senate Tribune met. The Palazzo Nuovo contains the **Capitoline Museum**, which is well known both for the wealth of material and for the fact that it is the oldest museum collection in the world. Begun by Sixtus IV, in 1471, it was enriched by popes Pius V, Clement XII (who opened it to the public), Benedict XIV, Clement XIII and Pius VI. Installed on two floors, the collection of the Capitoline Museum occupies practically all the rooms on the ground floor, as well as those on the upper floor, including the hall. Note should be taken on the first floor of the *Egyptian Collection* and, in the *Hall of Oriental Cults*, of an impressive series of statues, inscriptions, and reliefs. Treasures of classic art are contained in the other rooms on the ground floor (to the right of the atrium) and on the upper floor. In particular the monuments in the *Hall of Columns* and the *Hall of Emperors* (with *65 busts of Roman emperors*) come to mind as well as the *Hall of Philosophers*, the *Hall of the Faun*, and the famous *Hall of the Dying Gaul* (also called the *Dying Gladiator*).

MONUMENT TO VICTOR EMMANUEL II

After an extenuating competition, the realization of the monument was entrusted to Giuseppe Sacconi and was begun in 1885, to be finished and inaugurated in 1911. Its intentions were those of celebrating the splendor of the nation after the Unification of Italy, and with this in mind Sacconi envisioned it in imposing classicistic forms that would mirror the emotional and patriotic heart of the monument, the **Altar to the Homeland**, which was in turn envisioned as architecture within architecture with the solemn statue of *Rome* keeping watch over the **Tomb of the Unknown Soldier**. Note should also be taken of the *equestrian statue of Victor Emmanuel II*, for it is an integral part of the monument, also decidedly classicistic in style, as well as the fateful words from the Bulletin of Victory of Nov. 4, 1918.

Monument to Victor Emmanuel II with the « Altare della Patria ».

Trajan's Column.

IMPERIAL FORUMS

Although the Imperial Forums built near the precedent Forum of republican times, the underlying concept was more rational and grand. These enormous public squares (80-90,000 sq. meters) were enclosed by porticoes and an equestrian statue of the emperor was often to be found at the center while the square was shut off at the back by an imposing temple. The Imperial Forums were created with the hope of enhancing the prestige of the city and providing the citizens with a place for their markets, from which they could listen to harangues, and where they could participate in religious ceremonies. The first forum built was the **Forum Iulium** *(56-54 B.C.), under the auspices of Caesar himself. Next came the* **Forum of Augustus** *(32-31 B.C.), the* **Forum of Vespasian** *or of Peace (71-*

75), **Nerva's Forum** *(A.D. 98) and lastly* **Trajan's Forum** *(113). After the 6th century, the Forums were completely neglected and began gradually to be destroyed. During the Middle Ages a tiny portion was recuperated and a small district came into being which blended with the other Roman ruins. Most of it however became a mud-field and was rebaptized the zone of the « Pantani » or bogs, and the splendid buildings of Imperial times were destroyed or gravely damaged. Forgotten for centuries, the area was partially urbanized in the Renaissance but not until the 19th century and above all the 20th were the remains of this once magnificent architecture brought to light and the Via dei Fori Imperiali created.*

TRAJAN'S FORUM

Trajan's Forum extends northwards from Caesar's Forum and is oriented in the same direction. It is perpendicular to the forum of Augustus with which it borders on the west. The last and most imposing of the Imperial forums in Rome, it is the most important public work carried out by the emperor Trajan and his architect Apollodorus of Damascus. This imposing complex (300 m. long and 185 m. wide) was built between 106 and 113 A.D., financed by the proceeds of the Dacian war that had just been concluded.

The **Basilica Ulpia** which closed off the back of the square has also been excavated only in part. This is the largest basilica ever built in Rome, 17 meters long and almost 60 meters wide, taking its name from the family name of the emperor.

Trajan's Column stands in Trajan's Forum, between the two libraries, behind the Basilica Ulpia and in front of the temple of Divus Trajanus. Dedicated in A.D. 113, it is Doric; altogether it is almost 40 meters high, and at the top there was a statue of Trajan which was lost and replaced by one of *St. Peter* by Pope Sixtus V in 1587.

The column was meant to serve as the tomb of the emperor and the entrance in the base leads to an antechamber and then a large room which contained a golden urn with Trajan's ashes. The same door on the right leads to a spiral staircase of 185 steps, cut in the marble, which rises to the top of the column. A continuous frieze moves around the shaft of the column. About 200 meters long and varying in height from 90 to 125 centimeters, it represents Trajan's two victorious *Dacian campaigns* of A.D. 101-102 and 105-106, separated in the narration by a figure of *Victory* writing on a shield.

The **Temple of the Divus Trajanus** and of the Diva Plotina terminates the Forum to the northeast. It was built in A.D. 121 by Hadrian after Trajan's death. Not much is known about this temple which stood on the present site of the Church of S. Maria di Loreto and which must have been of colossal size with eight Corinthian columns on the front and eight on each side, over 20 meters high.

A section of the colonnade in Trajan's Forum.

The statue of Trajan placed in the Imperial Forums in modern times.

The ruins of the Temple of Mars Ultor in the Forum of Augustus.

A modern statue of Augustus erected in the Imperial Forums.

THE FORUM OF AUGUSTUS

The **Forum of Augustus** lies between the Forum of Caesar on the west and the *Suburra* district to the east. It was later enclosed on the north by the Forum of Trajan and to the south by the Forum Transitorium. It was constructed after costly expropriations on the part of the emperor so that he could free the area which was occupied by private dwellings. The entrance side, to the southwest, adjacent to the eastern side of Caesar's forum, is now under the Via dei Fori Imperiali as is the case with the front part of the square and the colonnades. There were also two secondary entrances at the back of the forum. The **Temple of Mars Ultor** consisted of a cella on a tall podium faced in marble, access to which was via a staircase with an altar at the center and two fountains at its outer edges. It had eight Corinthian columns over seventeen meters high on the front and eight on the long sides while the back was without (*peripteros sine postico*). The inside also had seven columns in two rows along the walls and at the back an apse with the cult statues of *Venus*, *Mars* and the *Divus Julius*.

12

The Roman Forum.

ROMAN FORUM

HISTORY

Situated in a valley between the Palatine, the Capitoline and the Esquiline hills, the area was originally a most inhospitable zone, swampy and unhealthy, until surprisingly modern reclamation work was carried out by the king Tarquinius Priscus, who provided the area with a highly developed drainage system (Cloaca Maxima). Once this complex reclamation work was finished, the Roman forum became a place for trade and barter. Numerous shops and a large square known as the market square were built and a zone was set apart for public ceremonies. It was here that the magistrates were elected, the traditional religious holidays were kept and those charged with various crimes were judged by a real court organization. After the Punic wars, thanks to the extraordinary development of the city, the urban fabric of the Forum took on a new look. As early as the 2nd century B.C., various basilicas — Porcia, Sempronia, and Aemilia — were built, the temples **of the Castors** and **of Concordia** were rebuilt, and the network of roads connecting the Forum to the quarters of the city continued to grow. After various transformations under the emperor Augustus, the Roman Forum became so large as to be considered the secular, religious, and commercial center of the city. After a period in which secular and political interests centered on other parts of the city, the Roman Forum reacquired its original prestige under Maxentius and Constantine who ordered the construction of the **Temple of Romulus** and the great **Basilica of Maxentius**. With the decadence of the Roman Empire, the splendid venerable structures of the Forum were severely damaged by the Barbarian invasions, especially the Goths (A.D. 410) and the Vandals (A.D. 455). The Roman Forum meanwhile became a place of worship for the early Christians who built the Churches of SS. Sergio e Bacco (on the **Via Sacra**), of S. Adriano (on the **Curia**), SS. Cosma e Damiano (**Temple of Peace**).

As time passed, the Forum was completely abandoned. What was left of the antique monuments was used by the people or demolished. During the Middle Ages the Forum became a pasture for sheep and cattle (hence its name of Campo Vaccino). For many centuries the prestige of the Roman Forum was a thing of the past. Not until the early 20th century was there a systematic re-evaluation of the area with excavation campaigns which lasted for various decades and which brought back to light the splendid evidence of the Rome of the kings as well as that of the republic and of the empire.

13

THE ARCH OF SEPTIMIUS SEVERUS

The arch is situated between the Rostra and the Curia and faces onto the square of the Roman Forum on the northeast. It was built in A.D. 203 to celebrate Septimius Severus' two Parthian campaigns of 195 and 197.

The arch is about 20 meters high, 25 meters wide and over 11 meters deep and has three passageways, a large one in the center and two smaller ones at the sides with short flights of steps leading up to them. On top is a tall attic with a monumental inscription which dedicates it to Septimius Severus and his son Caracalla. Representations of the monument on antique coins show that there was once a bronze quadriga with the emperors on the summit.

The arch is built of travertine and brick faced with marble. On the front are four columns standing on tall plinths decorated with reliefs of Roman soldiers and Parthian prisoners. The decoration includes two *Victories*, above *Genii of the Seasons*, which frame the central opening, and *Personifications of Rivers* for the side openings, with a small frieze with the *Triumphal Procession of the emperors* above. Gods are represented in the keystones: *Mars* twice for the principal arch and two female figures and two male figures, one of whom is *Hercules*, on the lesser arches.

But the most interesting part of the decoration is the series of four panels (m. 3.92x4.72) set above the side openings. The story of the two *Parthian campaigns* unfolds in a series of significant episodes. Each panel should be read from the bottom to the top, beginning with the left-hand panel on the side towards the Forum. Here are represented the phases of the first war, with the departure of the army from an encampment, a *Battle between Romans and Parthians* and the *Freeing of the city of Nisibis* to which the Parthians had laid siege, with the flight of their king Vologases and terminating with a scene of the *Emperor delivering a speech* to his army.

The south side of the Arch of Septimius Severus.

The second panel presents events from the second war: in the lower register the *Roman attack on Edessa* using war machines, including a large battering ram, and the *City opening its gates to surrender*; in the central band *Abgar*, king of Osrhoene, makes the *Act of submission to Septimius Severus* who harangues the army; in the upper tier is shown an imperial *Council of war* in a *castrum* and the *Departure* for enemy territory.

The third panel shows the *Attack on Seleucia*, a city on the Tigris, with the *Fleeing Parthians on horseback*, the *Submission of enemies* to the emperor and his *Entrance into the conquered city*.

And lastly the fourth panel shows the *Siege of the capital*, *Ctesiphon*, with war machines, and the flight from the city of the Parthian king Vologases and, in conclusion, the *Emperor's speech* before the conquered city.

THE TEMPLE OF SATURN

The temple was pseudoperipteral with Ionic columns on a high podium, situated southwest of the Rostra, on the slopes of the Capitoline hill.

It was one of the oldest temples in Rome and was erected in 497 B.C. but was completely rebuilt in 42 B.C. by the aedile L. Munazius Plancus. The large podium entirely faced in travertine, 40 meters long, 22.50 meters wide and 9 meters high, which is still extant dates to this phase. As indicated by the inscription on the architrave the temple was once more restored in A.D. 238 after a fire.

An avant-corps in front of the base consisted of two podia separated by a flight of stairs which led to the temple. One of these must have contained the headquarters of the Roman State Treasury. The threshold is still to be seen on the side facing the Forum.

The cella of the temple contained the statue of the god which was carried in procession for triumphal rites.

When this temple was built, Rome was passing through a particularly critical period due to extensive famines, epidemics and a severe economic and commercial crisis which characterized the years subsequent to the fall of the monarchy. Evidence of the sense of distress which took hold of the Roman people is the erection in these years of a number of temples: to Saturn in 497 B.C.; to Mercury, protector of commerce, in 495 B.C.; to Ceres, goddess of the earth and fertility, in 493 B.C.. The building of the Temple to Saturn must also be seen in this light for the god, before being identified with the Greek Chronos, was venerated for a particular characteristic known as « *Lua Saturni* », in other words the possibility of freeing the city from its afflictions.

The remains of the front of the Temple of Saturn.

THE TEMPLE OF CASTOR AND POLLUX

Facing on the square of the Roman Forum to the west of the Arch of Augustus, the temple is separated from the *Vicus Tuscus* by the east side of the Basilica of Gaius and Lucius. The temple was first built here in 484 B.C. and frequently rebuilt and enlarged. Its present aspect is that given to it by Tiberius in A.D. 6. The building was peripteral with eight Corinthian columns on its short sides and eleven on its long sides and with a cella on a concrete base (opus caementicium) (m. 50x30x7) which was originally faced with tufa blocks which were removed in modern times and reused.

The podium we now see dates to the restoration carried out by Metellius in 117 B.C., as do the stretches of black and white mosaic on the paving of the cella.

During the republican period, senate meetings were also held in the temple and after the middle of the 2nd century B.C. the podium also became a tribune for magistrates and orators in the legislative meetings that took place in this part of the forum square. It was from here that Caesar proposed his agrarian reforms. The building also became the headquarters for the office of weights and measures and during the period of the Empire part of the treasury of the tax office was kept in rooms in the long sides.

THE TEMPLE OF VESTA

The temple, which is one of the oldest in Rome, is situated to the south of the Via Sacra in front of the Regia. Its present appearance dates to A.D. 191, when it was restored (the last of many restorations) by Giulia Domna, wife of Septimius Severus. This was where the fire sacred to Vesta, the goddess of the household hearth, had to be kept perennially burning, for disaster threatened if the flame were to go out. This obviously meant the building was frequently in danger of fire.

The cult of Vesta goes back to the earliest days of Rome. According to tradition the mother of Romulus and Remus was a vestal virgin, and Livy refers that Numa Pompilius founded the order of the vestal priestesses charged with the care of the temple, establishing a retribution paid by the State and particular privileges. The building is circular and consists of a cella surrounded by twenty Corinthian columns set on a podium 15 meters in diameter faced with marble and with a staircase leading up to it on the east. The roof was conical with an opening for the smoke. The cella, which was articulated externally by engaged columns, contained no cult statue but only the hearth that was sacred to the goddess.

THE HOUSE OF THE VESTALS

The *Atrium Vestae*, on the south side of the Via Sacra, was a complex consisting of the Temple of Vesta and the house where the vestal virgins lived. As priestesses of the cult of Vesta, they were the custodians of the sacred hearth and were charged with performing the various rites involved. The only femine body of priests in Rome, the six vestal virgins were chosen among the children of patrician family between six and ten years old. They were required to stay in the order for thirty years, respecting a vow of chastity. On the other hand they enjoyed important privileges: they were subtracted from parental authority and the *patria potestas* passed to the Pontifex Maximus, they could travel in the city in a wagon (which was forbidden to women), they had reserved seats at the spectacles and ceremonies and could do as they best saw fit

The remains of the colonnade of the Temple of Castor and Pollux with a section of entablature.

with a sort of stipend they received from the State.

The entrance to the House of the Vestals is to the west, flanked by an aedicula which probably served as a lararium. It leads into a large rectangular central courtyard around which is a colonnade with eighteen columns on the long sides and six on the short sides, arranged in two orders.

The porticoes originally housed the statues which represented the *Virgines Vestales Maximae* (the senior members of the order), many of which have been found in the courtyard together with bases naming them in inscriptions which all date from the time of Septimius Severus on. Sone of the statues have been left here, arbitrarily arranged and on pedestals which do not belong to them.

The central part of the east side of the complex is comprised of the so-called « *tablinum* », a spacious hall that was originally vaulted, from which six rooms open off. They were also vaulted and are all about the same size (m. 4.15x3.50) which would lead one to think they were the rooms of the six vestal virgins. This group of rooms is generally thought to be the sanctuary of the Lares and is also where the *statue of Numa Pompilius* which has come down to us may originally have stood.

On the ground floor the south side has a series of service rooms set along a corridor — an oven, a mill, a kitchen, etc. Upstairs are the rooms of the vestals with baths. There must also have been a third floor.

The Temple of Vesta in the typical circular form.

The remains of the House of the Vestals with the statues of the senior members of this religious order.

THE BASILICA OF MAXENTIUS

Access to the Basilica of Maxentius, which stands outside the current archaeological zone of the Roman Forum, is from the Via dei Fori Imperiali. The building was begun in A.D. 308 by Maxentius and finished by Constantine, who modified the internal layout, shifting the entrance from the east to the south side, on the Via Sacra.

The building stands on a platform which is in part a substructure and which is superimposed on storerooms of considerable size, occupying an area of 100 by 65 meters. The entrance in the first plan, which Constantine also retained, opened into a narrow elongated atrium from which three openings led into the large central area, oriented east-west, 80 meters long, 25 meters wide and 35 meters high, covered by three cross vaults supported by eight columns in proconnesian marble, 14.50 meters high, set against piers (none of which are still *in situ*). At the back, right across from Maxentius' entrance, there was a semi-circular apse which contained an enormous acrolithic statue of Constantine (with the uncovered parts of the body in marble and the rest probably in gilded bronze), the head of which, 2.60 meters high, and a foot, two meters long, were found in 1487.

The aisles on either side of the nave were divided into three communicating bays with transversal coffered and stuccoed barrel vaults. Constantine's new project shifted the axis of the basilica from east-west to north-south, maintaining the tripartite division, with an entrance on the south side with four tall porphyry columns and a flight of steps which led from the Via Sacra to the floor of the building which was partly encased in the Velian hill. Across from this entrance a new semicircular apse was set into the wall at the center of the north aisle, preceded by two columns and with niches for statues framed by small columns on corbels.

The nave was illuminated by a series of large windows in the clerestory while the side aisles had two tiers of arched windows.

The ground plan and dimensions of the building were inspired by the imposing halls of the imperial baths, which were also called « *basilicas* ».

A view of the Basilica of Maxentius with, on the right, the Church of Santa Francesa Romana.

The Church of Santa Francesca Romana with its bell tower.

CHURCH OF SANTA FRANCESCA ROMANA

Built in the second half of the 10th century, the church was remodelled more than once in the course of time. The profiled white **facade** in travertine dates to the early 17th century and is by Carlo Lombardi who was extremely active in Rome at the time. The gabled facade is crowned by statues and has two orders of paired pilasters set on high stylobates. Above there is a large balcony and a porch with three arches.

The single nave **interior** has a fine coffered ceiling and a very old square of Cosmatesque mosaic in the pavement. At the back of the nave is an arch known as the Holy Arch, with a *Confessio* in polychrome marble by Bernini and a shrine with four columns which contains a fine marble group of *Saint Francesca Romana and an Angel* by Giosue Meli (1866). On the back wall of the right transept are two blocks of basalt,

protected by a gate, with two imprints which tradition says were made by Saint Peter when he knelt to pray here. On the left wall is the lovely *Funeral Monument of Gregory XI* by Olivieri. The apse is covered with mosaics depicting the *Madonna and Child with Saints Peter and Andrew*; on the high altar is the reputedly miraculous image of the *Madonna and Child* (12th cent.). Descending into the **crypt** we find the mortal remains of the saint at the altar and right across, a fine relief medallion of *Saint Francesca and an angel* by the school of Bernini. Lastly the, **Sacristy** houses rather fine paintings, including the panel of *Santa Maria Nova* (or the *Madonna del Conforto*) dating to the 5th century; a *Madonna Enthroned* by Sinibaldo Ibi from Perugia (1524); an imposing altarpiece, the *Miracle of St. Benedict*, by Subleyras, and various fine paintings by the school of Caravaggio. The adjacent **Convent** is the seat of the **Antiquarium Forense**.

The eastern side of the Arch of Titus.

THE ARCH OF TITUS

The arch rises in the eastern zone of the forums, south of the Temple of Venus and Roma.

The inscription on the side towards the Colosseum tells us that it was dedicated to the emperor Titus probably after his death in A.D. 81 by his brother and successor Domitian to commemorate the victory in the Judaic campaign of A.D. 70. The arch has a single passageway, and is 5.40 meters high, 13.50 meters wide and 4.75 meters deep, faced with pentelic marble (with piers in travertine restored by Valadier in 1822) and on the front and back it has four engaged columns with composite capitals. The decorative sculpture on the outside includes two figures of *Victories on globes and with banners* above the archivolt, the *Goddess Roma* and the *Genius of the Roman people*, on the keystones and a frieze in very high relief in the architrave with the *Triumph of Vespasian and Titus over the Jews*. Inside the arch a panel at the center of the coffered vault contains a relief with the *Apotheosis of Titus*. The panel on the north depicts a procession in which *Bearers of the lictor's fasces* precede the *Emperor who is being crowned by a Figure of Victory*; on the south side the *procession* as it passes through the *porta triumphalis* which is represented in a perspective view.

THE PALATINE

This is the most famous of Rome's hills and it retains the earliest memories of the old city. In fact the first groups of huts of the square city were built on the Palatine, before they spread over to the adjacent hills. Important public buildings, large temples and many private dwellings such as those of Cicero, Crassus and Tiberius Graccus went up here. Later the hill became the residence of the emperors of Rome who had their sumptuous palaces built here, including the **Domus Augustana**, the **Domus Flavia**, the **Domus Transitoria**, the **Domus Aurea**, and the **Domus Tiberiana**, of which considerable remains are still extant. The Palatine was then the residence of the Gothic kings and of many popes and emperors of the Western Empire; in the Middle Ages convents and churches were built. Finally in the 16th century most of the hill was occupied by the immense structures of **Villa Farnese** and the **Orti Farnesiani** (the first real botanical gardens). Archaeological excavation was begun in the 18th century and evidence of Rome's past was brought to light, including remnants of the **Domus Augustana**, the splendid paintings of republican period and the remains of the first dwellings that stood on the hill, as well as the imposing 16th-century entrance portal to the Orti Farnesiani.

Two stretches of the so-called Stadium of the Domus Augustana on the Palatine.

THE COLOSSEUM

The largest amphitheater ever built in Rome and a symbol for Romanism was the work of the Flavian emperors and was therefore called «Amphiteatrum Flavium». The name Colosseum first came to be used in the Middle Ages and can be traced to the nearby colossal bronze statue of Nero as the sun god which rose up from the site of the vestibule of the Domus Aurea.

The emperor Vespasian began the construction of the Colosseum in the valley between the Caelian, Palatine and Esquiline hills, on the site of the artificial lake around which Nero's royal residence was centered and which had been drained for the purpose. Vespasian's intentions were to restore to the Roman people what Nero had tyrannically deprived them of, as well as that of providing Rome with a large permanent amphitheater in place of the amphitheater of Taurus in the Campus Martius, a contemporary wooden structure erected by Nero after the fire of A.D. 64 but which was no longer large enough.

Work began in the early years of Vespasian's reign and in A.D. 79 the building, which had gone up only to the first two exterior orders with the first three tiers of steps inside, was dedicated. The fourth and fifth tiers were completed by Titus and it was inaugurated in A.D. 80 with imposing spectacles and games which lasted a hundred days. Under Domitian the amphitheater assumed its present aspect and size. According to the sources he added «ad clipea», in other words he placed the bronze shields which decorated the attic, adding the maenianum summum, the third internal order made of wooden tiers. Moreover he also had the subterraneans of the arena built, after which the naumachie (naval battles for which the arena had to be flooded) could no longer be held in the Colosseum, as we know from the sources.

Additional work was carried out by Nerva, Trajan and Antoninus Pius. Alexander Severus restored the building after it had been damaged by a fire caused by lightning in A.D. 217. Further restoration was carried out by Gordian III and later by Decius, after the Colosseum had once more been struck by lightning in A.D. 250. Other works of renovation were necessary after the earthquakes of A.D. 429 and 443. Odoacer had the lower tiers rebuilt, as witnessed by the inscriptions which we can read with the names of the senators dating from between 476 and 483 A.D. The last attempt at restoration was by Theodoric, after which the building was totally abandoned.

In the Middle Ages it became a fortress for the Frangipane and further earthquakes led to the material being used for new constructions. From the 15th century on it was transformed into a quarry for blocks of travertine until it was consecrated by Pope Benedict XV in the middle of the 18th century.

The building is elliptical in form and measures 188x156 meters at the perimeter and 86x54 meters inside, while it is almost 49 meters high. The external facade is completely of

◄ An aerial view of the Colosseum and the Forums.

The Colosseum.

A stretch of the cavea.

travertine and built in four stories. The three lower stories have 80 arches each, supported on piers and framed by attached three-quarter columns, Doric on the first floor, Ionic on the second and Corinthian on the third. They are crowned by an attic which functions as a fourth story, articulated by Corinthian pilasters set alternately between walls with a square window and an empty space which once contained the gilded shields. The beams which supported the large canopy (*velatium*) to protect the spectators from the sun were fitted into a row of holes between corbels. The canopies were unfurled by a crew of sailors from Misenum. The arches of the ground floor level were numbered to indicate the entrance to the various tiers of seats in the *cavea*. The four entrances of honor were situated at the ends of the principal axes of the building and were unnumbered, reserved for upper class persons of rank such as magistrates, members of religious colleges, the Vestal Virgins. The entrance on the north side was preceded by a porch (a small two-columned portico) which led to the imperial tribune through a corridor decorated with stuccoes.

The external arcades led to a twin set of circular corridors from which stairs led to the aisles (*vomitoria*) of the *cavea*; the second floor had a similar double ambulatory, and so did the third, but lower than the other two, while two single corridors were set one over the other at the height of the attic.

Inside, the *cavea* was separated from the arena by a podium almost four meters high behind which were the posts of honor. It was horizontally divided into three orders (*maenianum*) separated by walls in masonry (*baltei*). The first two *maeniana* (the second subdivided once more into upper and lower) had marble seats and were vertically articulated by the entrance aisles (*vomitoria*) and stairs. The result are circular sectors called *cunei*. It was therefore possible for the seats to be identified by the number of the tier, the cuneo and the seat. The third *maenianum* (or *maenianum summum*) had wooden tiers and was separated from the *maenianum secundum* below by a high wall. There was a colonnade with a gallery reserved for the women, above which a terrace served for the lower classes who had standing room only.

Access to seats in the *cavea* was based on social class, the higher up the seat the less important the person. The emperor's box was at the south end of the minor axis and this was also where consuls and Vestal Virgins sat. The box at the extremity was for the prefect of the city (« *praefectus Urbis* ») together with other magistrates. The tiers closest to the arena were reserved for senators. The inscriptions to be read on some of the extant tiers inform us that they were reserved for specific categories of citizens.

The arena was originally covered with wooden flooring which could be removed as required. In the case of hunts of ferocious animals the spectators in the *cavea* were protected by a metal grating surmounted by elephant tusks and with horizontally placed rotating cylinders so that it was impossible for the wild animals to climb up using their claws.

The area below the arena floor contained all the structures necessary for the presentation of the spectacles: cages for the animals, scenographic devices, storerooms for the gladiators' weapons, machines, etc. They were arranged in three annular walkways with openings that permitted the areas to be functionally connected with each other. A series of thirty niches in the outer wall was apparently used for elevators which took gladiators and beasts, up to the level of the arena.

The artificial basin created for the lake of the Domus Aurea was rationally exploited in the construction of the Colosseum, saving an enormous amount of excavation work. Once drained, the foundations were cast and travertine piers were set into a large elliptical concrete platform, forming a framework up to the third floor with radial walls in blocks of tufa and brick set between them. It was thus possible to work on the lower and upper parts at the same time, so that the building was subdivided into four sectors in which four different construction yards were engaged simultaneously.

Various types of spectacles were given in the Colosseum: the *munera* or contests between gladiators, the *vena-*

The model in the Museo della Civiltà Romana with the cross-section of the arena of the Colosseum, showing the cages and the underground passageways for the wild animals.

A Roman terracotta panel representing the arena with a scene of a hunt.

*A detail of the mosaics from Tusculum
in the Museo Borghese (3rd cent A.D.) representing a* venatio.

A stretch of the pavement of the road in front of the Colosseum.

tiones, or hunts of wild beasts and the previously cited *naumachie* which were soon transferred elsewheres because of the difficulty of flooding the arena of the amphitheater. Titus' reconstruction of the naval battle between Corinth and Corcyra in which 3000 men were employed was famous.

The gladiator contests took place in the form of a duel between opposing sides, generally until the death of one or the other. In the *venationes* those condemned to various penalties had to fight wild beasts and they were often unarmed. Records of the bloody outcome of these spectacles is to be found in the writings of ancient authors with reference to 10,000 gladiators and 11,000 wild beasts employed by Trajan on the occasion of his triumph over the Dacians or the impressive number of beasts in the hunts organized by Probus for his triumph.

Christians may or may not have been martyrized in the Colosseum. In A.D. 397 Honorius emanated an edict which prohibited gladiatorial games, but they were renewed under Valentinianus III. From A.D. 438 on, only hunts were allowed, which gradually diminished in importance until the last hunt held in A.D. 523 under Theodoric. A final point to consider is the number of spectators the Colosseum was capable of containing: opinions vary but the figure must have been around 50,000.

CONSTANTINE'S ARCH

The largest of the arches erected in Rome is on the route which the triumphal processions took in antiquity, between the Caelian and the Palatine hills. It is 21 meters high, almost 26 meters wide and over 7 meters deep, with three passageways, the central one of which is larger. It was built in A.D. 315 by decree of the Senate and the Roman people to celebrate the 10th anniversary of Constantine's ascent to the throne and his victory over Maxentius in the battle of Ponte Milvio in A.D. 312. The decoration of the arch employed a number of reliefs and sculpture from other monuments. The four detached marble columns on each of the principal sides, surmounted by eight statues of Dacians, are in *pavonazzetto* marble (white with purple veining, from Asia Minor) and date to Trajan's time. Eight tondos about two meters in diameter of Hadrian's period are set in pairs over the side passageways, inserted into porphyry slabs. Four *Scenes of the hunt* are represented, and four *Sacrificial scenes*. The figure of Hadrian appears in each scene, even though his head has been replaced by that of Constantine. On the attic, on either side of the inscription which is repeated both on the front and the back of the monument, are eight reliefs from the period of Marcus Aurelius, also set in pairs, which probably came from an honorary arch. They form a cycle which celebrates the *Return of the emperor* in A.D. 173 after his campaigns against the Marcomanni and the Quadi, in a series of exemplary episodes which correspond to scenes presented in the Aurelian column. A marble frieze from Trajan's time has been reused and cut into four parts, two of which are on the short sides of the attic and two on the interior of the central passage. The scenes have to do with Trajan's two *Dacian campaigns* (A.D. 101-102 and 105-106). The decorative parts which date to the building of the arch comprise the reliefs at the bases of the columns, the keystones of the arches and, on the short sides, medallions with the *Sun God* and the *Goddess of the Moon* on a chariot. The most important part of Constantine's decoration is the large historical frieze set above the lesser openings, and which continues on the short sides of the arch with episodes from the *Military Deeds of Constantine*.

The Arch of Constantine.

THE CIRCUS MAXIMUS

Now only the lay of the land, much higher than the original arena, betrays the form of the original structure. For a long time it was built entirely of wood. In 329 B.C. the *carceres* or stalls for the horses and chariots were built in painted wood, as well as the *spina* in the center which covered and channeled the stream which ran through the valley and around which the race was run.

In 174 B.C. the censors Fulvius Flaccus and Postumius Albinus had the *carceres* built in masonry, and placed seven stone eggs along the spina as markers for the number of circuits the chariots had run. In 33 B.C. Agrippa had bronze dolphins set up for the same scope. Caesar also used the Circus for hunts. On the side towards the Palatine, Augustus had the *pulvinar*, a sacred box reserved for the tutelary gods of the games, set up and in 10 B.C. he had the obelisk of Ramsetes II taken at Heliopolis placed on the spina. The obelisk, 23.70 meters high, was transferred to Piazza del Popolo by Pope Sixtus V in 1587.

Claudius took a hand in the restoration after a fire in A.D. 36. He had the *carceres* rebuilt in marble and had the *metae* (the goals, conical extremes of the *spina*) covered in gilded bronze. The Circus was once more destroyed in the fire of A.D. 64. Nero rebuilt it and increased the number of seats. Another fire under Domitian ravaged the building and reconstruction was finished by Trajan.

Constantine restored it and Constantius II embellished the *spina* with a second obelisk of Tuthmosis II, which came from Thebes and was even higher than the other one (32.50 m.) and which Pope Sixtus V had placed in Piazza San Giovanni in Laterano in 1587.

The Circus measured 600x200 meters and had a capacity of 320,000 spectators who watched the chariot races that were held there. The most important were those of the *Ludi Romani* the first week of September, which opened with a religious procession in which the highest religious and civil authorities of the city took part.

THEATER OF MARCELLUS

The project for the so-called theater of Marcellus dates to Caesar's time, but the building was finished in 13 B.C. by Augustus who officially dedicated it in the name of his nephew Marcellus, his first designated heir, who died early in 23 B.C. In the 13th century the building was occupied by the noble Savelli family; in the 18th century it passed to the Orsini. The fine Renaissance palace that occupies the third floor of the exterior facade of the *cavea* is the work of the architect Baldassarre Peruzzi.

A view of the Circus Maximus today.

Part of the structures of the Theater of Marcellus.

The theater must have been built on powerful sub-structures, and the front was provided with a facade of 41 arches, framed by engaged columns, on three floors. The first two floors are Doric and Ionic orders, the third, of which nothing remains, must have been an attic closed by Corinthian pilasters. It was originally 32.60 m. high.

It has been calculated that the *cavea* (diam. 129.80 m.) could hold between 15 and 20,000 spectators, making it the largest theater in Rome as far as audience capacity was concerned. Beyond the orchestra (diam. 37 m.) was the stage, of which nothing remains. On either side were apsed halls, of which a pier and a column of one are still standing. Behind the stage was a large semi-circular exedra with two small temples. The building was also noticeable for its rich decoration, still visible in the Doric frieze on the lower order.

ISOLA TIBERINA

According to an old written tradition, the small island in the Tiber now known as Isola Tiberina was formed when the grain that had been harvested in the Campus Martius (private property of the Tarquins) was thrown into the river after the expulsion of the Etruscan kings from Rome.

The first important building erected on the island dates to 291 B.C. This was the temple of Aesculapius.

Nothing remains today of the original building but the site is probably that of the 17th-century **Church of S. Bartolomeo**, and the well that still exists near the altar could correspond to the sacred fount. The porticoes of the sanctuary of Aesculapius were a real hospital. Numerous inscriptions preserved mention miraculous healings or dedications to the god. In the Middle Ages the island continued to be set aside as a hospital, thanks in part to its being isolated from the inhabited areas, and it is still used as such with the **Hospital of the Fatebenefratelli**, adjacent to the small **Church of S. Giovanni Calibita**.

In antiquity the island was also joined to the city by two bridges. The one which still today connects it to the left bank, near the theater of Marcellus, is the ancient **Pons Fabricius**. The Pons Fabricius is 62 m. long and 5.50 m. wide; the two large slightly flattened arches have a span of 24.50 m. and spring from a massive central pier, which is pierced by a small arch that serves to relieve the pressure of the water on the structure during floods.

The other bridge which joins the island to Trastevere is no longer the original one. The Pons Cestius was torn down between 1888 and 1892. It had been built in the first century B.C., perhaps by the praetor of 44 B.C., the same C. Cestius to whom the famous funeral monument in the shape of a pyramid is dedicated. In A.D. 370 it was restored by emperor Valentinian I.

The unique form of the Isola Tiberina in the shape of an elongated boat, together with the remembrance of the ship which had brought the serpent of Aesculapius to Rome, gave rise to an odd architectural adaptation of the site which probably dates to the first century. The easternmost point of the island was turned into the prow of a trireme.

The Isola Tiberina and the Ponte Rotto.

PIAZZA NAVONA

The most famous square of Baroque Rome stands on the site of Domitian's stadium and the name seems to derive from a popular corruption of the term for the competitive games « *in agone* » which were held here. From the times of Domitian on, the place was used almost exclusively for sports events, including the famous August regatta in which the participants wore the colors of the nobles and the civic clergy. Even now the feast of the *Befana* (the Italian version of Santa Claus who arrives on January 6th) is celebrated there in January with a typical market. But the real attraction of the square is the famous **Fountain of the Four Rivers** by Gian Lorenzo Bernini, dated 1651, and thanks to which the artist gained the admiration and protection of the pope then in office, Innocent X. The rivers represented in the fountain are the *Danube*, the *Ganges*, the *Nile*, the *Rio de la Plata*. They are arranged on a steep rocky reef from which a Roman obelisk taken from the Circus of Maxentius rises up into the air. In line with the Fountain of the Four Rivers are the **Fountain of the Moor**, in front of the **Palazzo Pamphili**, and the **Fountain of Neptune**, formerly of the *Calderari*, at the northern end of the square.

Piazza Navona: the square with the Church of Sant'Agnese in Agone.

30

The front of the Pantheon and a view of the interior and the dome.

PANTHEON

The first building was erected in 27 B.C. by Marcus Vipsanius Agrippa, the faithful advisor of Augustus.

In Trajan's time, the temple was completely rebuilt by Hadrian between 118 and 128, in the form we still see today. The inscription on the frieze of the porch, *M(arcus) Agrippa L(uci) f(ilius) co(n)s(ul) tertrium fecit*, was therefore placed there by Hadrian who never put his own name on any of the monuments he built.

Hadrian's reconstruction profoundly modified the original building. The facade was set facing north, the porch was set on the site occupied by the original temple and the large rotunda coincided with the open area in front. Still today the large columned porch has a facade composed of eight columns in grey granite. Two red granite columns each are set behind the first, third, sixth, and eighth column of the facade, thus forming three aisles. The central aisle, which is the widest, leads to the entrance. The side aisles end in two large niches destined for the statues of Agrippa and Augustus. The tympanum was decorated with a crowned eagle in bronze of which only the fix-holes still remain. The ceiling of the porch was also decorated in bronze but this was removed by Pope Urban VIII Barberini (which lies at the root of the famous pasquinade: « *quod non fecerunt barbari, fecerunt Barberini* »).

Behind the porch is a massive construction in brick, which joins it to the Rotonda, a gigantic cylinder with a wall that is six meters thick, divided into three superposed sectors, marked externally by cornices. The wall gets lighter as it rises, and the thickness of the walls, with brick vaulting in various places, is not always completely solid. The height of the Rotonda to the top of the dome is precisely that of its diameter (43.30 m.) so that the interior space is a perfect sphere. The dome is a masterpiece of engineering: it is the largest dome ever covered by masonry and it was cast in a single operation on an imposing wooden centering.

The **interior** of the building has six distyle niches at the sides and a semicircular exedra at the back, with eight small aedicules in between which have alternating arched and triangular pediments. The dome is decorated with five tiers of lacunar coffering except for a smooth band near the oculus, the circular opening (9 m. diam.) which illuminates the interior.

COLUMN OF MARCUS AURELIUS

Set at the center of Piazza Colonna, it was named after the emperor Marcus Aurelius, who had it erected between 189 and 196 in honor of his victories over the Marcomanni, the Quadi and the Sarmatians. Almost 30 meters high, the shaft is enveloped by a bas-relief spiral, which, like the one on Trajan's Column, narrates the events of the Germanic and Sarmatian wars. The statue of *Saint Paul* on the top was set there by Domenico Fontana in 1588 and replaced the one of Marcus Aurelius once there.

The site was originally in the heart of the imperial Rome of the Antonines, between the Temple of Marcus Aurelius and the Temple of Hadrian.

Now the column rises in Piazza Colonna with a base restored by Fontana who, as shown by the inscription, erroneously thought it had been dedicated to Antoninus Pius. The interior of the column is hollow and a spiral staircase of 190 steps leads to the top.

TREVI FOUNTAIN

It may or may not be the most beautiful fountain in Rome but it is without doubt the most famous. The imaginative concept, the theatrical composition, the sober and imposing beauty of the sculptured marble figures make it a true masterpiece both of sculpture and of architecture. Pietro da Cortona and above all Bernini, who began the undertaking, both had a hand in the project. The death of Pope Urban VIII brought work to a standstill and it was not until about a hundred years later that Clement XII entrusted the work to Nicola Salvi, who finished the undertaking between 1732 and 1751.

The Column of Marcus Aurelius.

The Trevi Fountain.

Detail of one of the tritons guiding the horses of Neptune.

The fountain is highly symbolic with intellectual connotations. A tall and sober *Arch of Triumph* (the palace of Neptune) dominates the scene from on high. It is comprised of an order of four Corinthian columns and is surmounted by an attic with statues and a balustrade. A large niche at the center of the arch lends balance and symmetry to the whole ensemble. A smaller niche to the left contains the statue of *Abundance* by F. Valle, and above this is a fine relief depicting *Agrippa approving the plans for the Aqueduct* by Andrea Bergondi. The niche on the right contains the figure of *Salubrity*, also by F. Valle, with a relief above of the *Virgin showing soldiers the Way*, by G. B. Grossi.

The central niche seems to impart movement to the imposing figure of *Neptune* who firmly guides a chariot drawn by sea horses, known as the « *agitated* » horse and the « *placid horse* », names obviously derived from the way in which the two animals have been represented. As they gallop over the water, the horses are guided in their course by fine figures of *tritons* which emerge from the water and which were sculptured by P. Bracci in 1762. The setting all around consists of rocks.

The Barcaccia Fountain.

The Spanish Steps.

PIAZZA DI SPAGNA AND TRINITÀ DEI MONTI

One of the most characteristic squares in the city, the **Piazza di Spagna**, stretches out for over 270 meters, divided into two triangular areas. It is surrounded by outstanding buildings, such as the **Palazzo di Propaganda Fide**, seat of the *Congregation of Propaganda Fide* instituted by Pope Gregory XV in 1622. The facade on the square is by Bernini (1644) and is articulated in three floors. The sober, elegant design is in brick. The more complex facade at the side however is by Borromini (1665) and is concave in the center. It is articulated by pilaster strips which reach up to the first floor where unique concave windows are set off by columns and pilasters. The large portal leads to the vestibule with, nearby, Borromini's **Church of the Magi** (dei Re Magi) (1666). The restrained luminous interior has a fine *Adoration of the Magi* by Giacinto Gemignani (1643). Another noteworthy complex is the **Palazzo di Spagna** built by A. Del Grande in 1647 which has an important facade with lovely portals tied together by severe rustication. The square is centered on the **Barcaccia Fountain**, by Pietro Bernini (1627-1629), an ingenious and lively representation of a large boat which is sinking and spouting water from both stern and prow. Piazza di Spagna is where the famous **Spanish Steps (Scalinata di Trinità dei Monti)** begin. Built entirely in travertine by Francesco De Sanctis (1723-1726) the twelve flights of steps of

varying widths branch off into various blocks as they move upward towards the Piazza Trinità dei Monti. At the center of the square is the *Sallustian Obelisk* which comes from the Sallustian Gardens. The square is dominated by the powerful structures of the **Church of Trinità dei Monti**, one of the most imposing Franciscan churches in the city. Begun in 1503 at the request of Louis XII, the church has been remodelled at various times. The sober facade, by Carlo Maderno, with a single order of pilasters and a broad portal with columns and a large balustrade, is preceded by a staircase by Domenico Fontana that is decorated with capitals and antique bas-reliefs. The interior has a single large nave and contains fine works of art including a lovely fresco with *Stories of St. John the Baptist* by Naldini, in the first chapel on the right; Daniele da Volterra's famous and brilliant *Assumption*, in the third chapel on the right. The second chapel on the left contains the *Deposition*, another masterpiece by Daniele da Volterra, and in the sixth chapel on the left, Perin del Vaga's *Assumption* and *Isaiah and Daniel* (on the front of the tomb), Taddeo Zuccari's *Death of Maria* and the *Assumption* by Federico and Taddeo Zuccari. Another outstanding work by Federico Zuccari, the *Coronation of the Virgin*, is in the chapel to the left of the presbytery. The **Cloister** contains frescoes by various artists with *Stories from the life of Saint Francis of Paola*.

The Palazzo di Giustizia.

Piazza del Popolo.

PALAZZO DI GIUSTIZIA

Built between 1889 and 1910 to designs by Guglielmo Calderini, the court building is characterized by the fact that the central block is higher than those on either side (3 floors), as well as by its imposing dimensions. The architecture is also accompanied by typical examples of monumental sculpture, such as the large *Quadriga* by Ettore Ximenes which crowns the principal block, the enormous statues (almost the equivalent of antique colossi) of the *Jurists* on the entrance ramps, the group with *Justice*, *Force* and the *Law* on the central portal.

PIAZZA DEL POPOLO

Piazza del Popolo, one of the most characteristic areas of neoclassical Rome, is the child of Giuseppe Valadier's creative genius in the field of town planning and architecture, a project he began work on in 1793.

It is distinguished by the low exedras which define the boundaries of the square and which are topped by statues of the *Four Seasons*, while the center is emphasized by the two fountains, *Neptune and the Tritons* and *Rome between the Tiber and the Aniene River*. All the sculpture mentioned above dates to the first half of the 19th century and was made respectively by Gnaccarini, Laboureur, Stocchi, Baini, Ceccarini.

VILLA BORGHESE

First created for Cardinal Caffarelli Borghese early in the 17th century, the park was completely renewed at the end of the 18th century by the architects Asprucci and the painter Unterberger, but what we see now was the work of Luigi Canina at the beginning of the 19th century.

Generously donated to the city of Rome in 1902 by Umberto I, King of Italy, it was supposed to have been called after him. However, notwithstanding official names, it is still known as Villa Borghese in honor of the man who founded it.

This is the largest park in Rome with a perimeter of six kilometers and it is also the loveliest with a wealth of trees and charming paths. Entrance is from the overpass of the Viale dell'Obelisco, but also from the Porta Pinciana, Piazzale Flaminio and other minor entrances.

The Temple of Aesculapius in Villa Borghese.

The Casino Borghese.

The Emperors Gallery in the Museo Borghese.

MUSEO AND GALLERIA BORGHESE

One of the most prestigious collections of sculpture and painting in the world is housed in the fine building known as the Casino Borghese, built for Cardinal Scipione Borghese by Giovanni Vasanzio (1613-1615). The Museum is installed on the ground floor and the itinerary leads through a portico, the Salone, and eight rooms, with various masterpieces by Bernini and Canova as well as examples of marble sculpture from Roman times. The Gallery, installed on the upper floor, has a spacious vestibule and twelve rooms and a selection of paintings which are truly priceless. A brief survey of the two famous collections follows.

Museo Borghese: **Portico**: sculpture from the Roman period and two panels of sarcophagi which depict the Muses. **Salone**: twelve *busts* in colored marble by G. B. della Porta (16th cent.) are in the niches; the vaults were frescoed by Martino Rossi in the second half of the 18th century (*Camillus breaking off negotiations with Brennus* and the *Allegory of Glory*); the pavement contains five fragments of third-century mosaics (scenes of gladiators and the hunt). From the left, various pieces of antique sculpture (*Isis*, the *Satyr*, *Augustus*, a *Faun*, *Hadrian*, *Bacchus*, *Antoninus Pius*); **Room I** (Sala della Paolina): the decoration on the vault and walls (*Judgement of Paris* and *Stories of Aeneas*) by D. De Angelis; the highlight

at the center of the room is *Pauline Borghese as Venus Victrix (1805)* by Canova, strikingly beautiful in its softly modeled forms and dominated by a subtle tempting sensuousness. *Room II* (of David): the frescoes in the vault are by Caccianiga (*Fall of Phaethon*); the five niches in the room contain five late Roman *busts*; but what most strikes the eye is the dynamic sculpture of *David*, an early work by Gian Lorenzo Bernini (1623-1624), at the center of the room. Around it are various Roman *statues*. **Room III** (of Apollo and Daphne). The fresco in the vault depicts the *Death of Daphne* by Pietro Angeletti. At the center is Bernini's wonderful sculpture of *Apollo and Daphne*, a bold and innovative work of 1624; the surrounding statues are Roman. **Chapel**: the walls are lined with *frescoes* by Deruet and Lanfranco; particularly noteworthy is a *female head with serpents* dating to the 5th century B.C. **Emperors' Gallery** (**Room IV**) with eighteen *Busts of Emperors* in porphyry and alabaster (17th cent.). The *Story of Galathea* is represented in the vault, at the center is the *Rape of Proserpine*, another example of Bernini's complex sculpture (1622); of particular note otherwise are the statues of *Dionysius* and the *Marine Venus*. **Room V** (of the Hermaphrodite): in the vault *Hermaphrodite and Salmace* by Buonvicini; the Roman mosaic in the pavement has fishing scenes; of note the statue of the *Sleeping Hermaphrodite*, a reproduction of a Hellenistic original. **Room VI** (of Aeneas and Anchises): in the vault:

the *Council of the Gods*, by Pacheux; at the center the marble group of *Aeneas and Anchises* by Gian Lorenzo and Pietro Bernini. The most striking piece on one side, among other Roman works, is *Truth unveiled by Time*, another important work by Bernini (1652). **Room VII** (Egyptian room): in the vault *frescoes* by T. Conca, in the pavement three Roman *mosaics*; the most striking of the other Roman statues is the *Youth on a Dolphin*, a copy of a Hellenistic original. **Room VIII** (of the Dancing Faun): in the vault, the *Sacrifice to Silenus* by T. Conca and, at the center, the *Dancing Faun*, a Roman copy of a Hellenistic original.

Galleria Borghese: **Vestibule**: housed here are the *Three Ages of Man*, painted by Sassoferrato, as well as works by Luca Cambiaso and Rutilio Manetti. **Room IX**: in the vault the *Stories of Aeneas* by A. De Maron (1786), particularly of note among the other works are the *Deposition*, one of Raphael's Roman masterpieces; the *Portrait of a Man* and the *Portrait of a Lady with a Unicorn*, also by Raphael; the crystalline *Madonna and Child*, the *young Saint John and Angels* by Botticelli; the imposing *Holy Family* by Fra Bartolomeo, Perugino's *Madonna* and other works by Andrea del Sarto, Lorenzo di Credi, Santi di Tito, Mariotto Albertinelli, Pinturicchio. **Room X**: striking are the *Madonna and Child with the young St. John* by Andrea del Sarto, and Bronzino's dramatic *St. John the Baptist*; also works by Luca Cranach, Berreguete, Sodoma and Rosso Fiorentino. **Room XI**, with Lorenzo Lotto's *Madonna and Child with Saints* and his *Self Portrait*; of partic-

ular note, as well as works by Savoldo, Palma il Vecchio, and Bernini. **Room XII**: contains works by Annibale Carracci, Domenichino, Pietro da Cortona. **Room XIII**: contains works by Giulio Romano, Puligo, Scipione Pulzone, Franciabigio. **Room XIV**: in the vault the *Council of the Gods* by Lanfranco. Particular mention among the works exhibited goes to the *David with the head of Goliath*, the *Madonna of the Serpent* (painted for the Palafrenieri), and *St. John the Baptist in the Desert*, three sublime paintings by Caravaggio; there are also works by A. Carracci, Guercino, and some realistic sculpture by Bernini. **Room XV**: in the vault, *Allegory of Aurora* by D. Corvi. **Room XVI**: in the ceiling, *Flora* by G. B. Marchetti; the room is almost completely dedicated to the works of Iacopo Bassano. **Room XVII**: in the vault, *Story of Walter of Angers* by G. Cades; as well as works by Dossi, Garofalo, Scarsellino, Francia. **Room XVIII**: in the vault, *Jupiter and Antiope* by G. Gagneraux; outstanding are many paintings by Rubens, his famous *Susannah and the Elders* and the *Deposed Christ* and some paintings by Mandekens, Brill, Sustris, and other Flemish artists. **Room XIX**: among the many works exhibited in this room mention must be made of Correggio's touching and intimate *Danae* and various paintings by Dossi, Pordenone, Parmigianino. **Room XX**: here are some of Titian's masterpieces, such as *Sacred and Profane Love*, *Venus Blindfolding Cupid*, and *St. Domenic*; Antonello da Messina's profoundly introspective *Portrait of a Man* and works by Veronese, Bellini and Carpaccio.

Pauline Borghese by Canova.

Castel Sant'Angelo.

CASTEL SANT'ANGELO

Castel S. Angelo, whose imposing mass still dominates the panorama of Rome, and which is known as the *Mole Adriana*, was not originally built for defensive purposes but as the funeral monument of the emperors. A new bridge (called Pons Aelius from the *nomen* of the emperor) which still exists as **Ponte S. Angelo** was built to put the monument in communication with the Campus Martius. This bridge flanks Nero's bridge, further downstream. It consisted of three large central arches and two inclined ramps supported by three smaller arches on the right bank and two on the left bank.

Most of the structural parts of the Mausoleum, which was incorporated into Castel S. Angelo in the Middle Ages, have been preserved. The building consisted of an enormous quadrangular basement, 89 m. per side and 15 m. high. On top was a cylindrical drum (diam. 64 m., height 21 m.) flanked by radial walls. A tumulus of earth planted with trees rose up over the drum. Along the edges were decorative marble statues and at the center, raised even higher up, was a podium with columns on top of which was a bronze quadriga with the statue of Hadrian. The exterior of the enclosure was faced with Luni marble and with inscriptions of the *tituli* of the personages buried in the monument; engaged pilasters were set at the corners and the upper part was decorated with

a frieze of garlands and bucrania (fragments are preserved in the Museo del Castello). The drum was faced on the outside with travertine and fluted pilaster strips. The entire monument was enclosed in a wall with bronze gates, decorated with peacocks (two are in the Vatican), perhaps a funerary symbol.

The original entrance to the tomb, with three openings, was on the side of the base that faces the river. The current entrance is at least three meters higher up. From here a corridor (*dromos*) led to a square vestibule with a semicircular alcove on the back wall, faced with yellow Numidian marble. The helicoidal gallery which rises ten meters and leads to the funeral chamber begins to the right of the vestibule. The vault of this corridor, with four vertical light wells, is in rubblework; the pavement still retains traces of its original mosaic decoration while the walls were covered with marble to a height of three meters. The funeral chamber, right at the center of the massive drum, is square (3 m. per side) with three rectangular niches; illumination is from two oblique windows in the vault. The cinerary urns of the emperors were placed in this room. Above the funerary chamber were two superposed cellae which by means of an annular corridor led to the top of the monument.

As early as A.D. 403 the emperor Honorius may have incorporated the building in an outpost bastion of the Aurelian walls. In 537, when it was already a fortress, it was attacked by Vitiges and his Goths. In the 10th century it was transformed into a castle. Its appearance today is that of a massive fortress on a square base and with circular **towers** at the four corners (known as the towers of **St. Matthew**, **St. John**, **St. Mark**, and **St. Luke**) onto which a circular body has been grafted. This was built following the lines of the Imperial mausoleum under Benedict IX. Further work was ordered by Alexander VI and by Julius II who had the south loggia above the papal apartments added.

At the summit is the panoramic terrace, watched over by the *Angel* about to fly off, which seems to be why the building is called as it is, for the winged messenger is said to have saved Rome from a terrible plague at the time of Gregory the Great.

Inside the castle-fortress are the rooms of the **Museo Nazionale Militare** and of **Art**.

Two views of the Ponte Sant'Angelo over the Tiber river.

VATICAN CITY

HISTORICAL SKETCH

Vatican City spreads out to the right of the Tiber and lies between Monte Mario to the north and the Janiculum to the south. Of old the area now covered by the small Vatican State was called Ager Vaticanus *and it was occupied by a circus and Nero's gardens. Since 1929, the year in which the Lateran Treaty was stipulated between the Holy See and the Italian State, the Vatican City has been an independent sovereign state and it contains exceedingly important examples of art and architecture. The boundaries of this state, whose residents can be numbered in the hundreds, is defined by the Via Porta Angelica, Piazza del Risorgimento, Via Leone IV, the Viale Vaticano, Via della Sagrestia, and the Piazza San Pietro. The Pope, in addition to being the head of the Apostolic Roman Catholic Church, has full legislative, executive and judiciary powers. The Vatican State is completely independent of the Italian State, even though they maintain extremely friendly relations. The Vatican prints its own stamps, has its own railroad station, and a well-known newspaper, the Osservatore Romano, which is distributed throughout Italy. The city also has its own police force (once called Pontifical Gendarmes) and a real police service as represented by the famous « Swiss Guards » which, from the early 16th century, protected the person of the pope and still today wear uniforms that were probably designed by Michelangelo.*

PIAZZA SAN PIETRO

The fact, alone, that the great and truly unique Basilica of St. Peter's in Vatican faces out on this square would make it perhaps the most widely known of Roman piazzas. But above and beyond this, the space itself merits attention for its size (an enormous ellipse whose greatest diameter measures 240 m.) and the brilliant project by Gian Lorenzo Bernini whose scope was that of singling out this square from all others through the use of the imposing porticoes.
These porticoes are arranged in semicircles along the short sides of the square and consist of four parallel rows of Tuscan-Doric columns which provide a choice of three paths. Above

The facade of the Basilica of San Pietro.

The statues towering above Bernini's porticoes.

Next pages, Piazza San Pietro with Bernini's porticoes and the obelisk viewed from the Basilica.

the canonic entablature are 140 colossal statues of *Saints*, as well as the insignia of the patron pope, Alexander VII. At the center of the square, the plain obelisk, flanked by two fountains, stands at the crossing of the two diameters of the ellipse. Termed « aguglia » (needle) in the Middle Ages, the *obelisk* came from Heliopolis and was brought to Rome by the emperor Caligula, and set on the spina of Nero's Circus, which is where St. Peter's in Vatican now stands. Throughout the various phases of restoration, destruction, and reconstruction, the « aguglia » stayed next to the Basilica and was not set up at the center of the square until 1586 by Domenico Fontana, who also saw to the engineering aspect of the undertaking. The other architect, Carlo Fontana, designed the left-hand *fountain* in Piazza San Pietro, built in 1677 as a *pendant* to the one on the right designed by Carlo Maderno about fifty years earlier. A curious fact concerning the obelisk mentioned above is that it was used, or was believed to have been used in the Middle Ages, as a reliquary for the ashes of Caesar, and then (up to now) for a fragment of the Holy Cross.

BASILICA OF SAN PIETRO IN VATICANO

In the classical period the site was occupied by Nero's Circus, between the Tiber, the Janiculum, and the Vatican hill, and St. Peter, the Prince of the Apostles, was martyred and then buried here.
Pope Anacletus had already had a small basilica, *ad corpus*,

or a simple shrine built here. In 324 the emperor Constantine replaced the presumably modest shrine with a basilica of Constantinian type, in line with the other churches built in Rome in that period. Finished in 349 by Constantius, son of Constantine, the original St. Peter's was enriched throughout the centuries by donations and updatings by the popes and munificent princes. It was in Constantine's basilica that Charlemagne received the crown from the hands of Leo III in 800 and after him Lothair, Louis II, and Frederick III were crowned emperors. Even so, a thousand years after its foundation St. Peter's was falling into ruin and it was Nicholas V, on the advice of Leon Battista Alberti and with a plan by Bernardo Rossellino, who began to renovate and enlarge the Basilica. Various parts of the building were torn down, and work on the new tribune was started but soon came to a halt when Nicholas V died. Work was not resumed until 1506 when Julius II della Rovere was pope. Most of the original church was dismantled by Bramante (who earned himself the title of « maestro ruiante »), with the intention of building ex novo a « modern » building in the classic style: a Greek-cross plan inspired by the Pantheon. Various supervisors succeeded each other until about the middle of the century: Fra Giocondo, Raphael, Giuliano da Sangallo, Baldassarre Peruzzi, Antonio da Sangallo the Younger, and, finally, Michelangelo, who needless to say interpreted Bramante's plan, modifying it in part, and envisioned the great dome (originally hemispherical) which crowned the renovated basilica. Michelangelo was succeeded by Vignola, Pirro

The interior of Saint Peter's.

The celebrated bronze baldacchino *by Bernini.*

Ligorio, Giacomo Della Porta, Domenico Fontana, all of whom interpreted his ideas quite faithfully. Then under Paul V, it was decided to reinstate the basilica plan, and return to the Latin-cross idea. With this in mind, the architect Carlo Maderno added three chapels to each side of the building and brought the nave as far as the present facade, the building of which was entrusted to him when he won an important competition. Work was begun in November of 1607 and terminated in 1612, after having « employed mountains of travertine from Tivoli ».

The **facade**, which is truly imposing in its proportions, is based on the use of the giant Corinthian order, which articulates the front of the building with columns and pilasters. On the ground floor these frame a large central porch, with an arch on either side (the one on the left, the so-called *Arch of the Bells*, leads to Vatican City), and, above, a row of nine balconies. The crowning element is a canonic attic surmounted by a balustrade which supports thirteen enormous statues, representing all the *Apostles*, except for St. Peter, as well as *Christ* and *St. John the Baptist*. Above all looms **Michelangelo's imposing dome** with its strong ribbing, and, emerging from the front but to the side, the « minor » domes of the Gregoriana and the Clementina chapels by Giacomo Barozzi da Vignola. After the death of Carlo Maderno in 1629, the next director of works, Gian Lorenzo Bernini, left his un-

mistakeable mark. The prevalently Baroque character the building now displays was his doing. It is sufficient to mention the decorative transformation of the nave and the aisles, the erection of the justly famous bronze *baldacchino* (begun in 1624 and inaugurated on St. Peter's day in 1633), the decoration of the piers of the dome with four large statues, the installment at the back of the apse of the *Throne of St. Peter*, one of Bernini's most sumptuous inventions, a truly marvelous machine, built around the old wooden chair which a pious tradition says was used by the apostle Peter. The organization of St. Peter's square, once more by Bernini, also dates to the papacy of Alexander VII (who financed the works for the throne), while under Clement X the architect designed and built the small round temple which comprises the shrine of the Chapel of the Sacrament.

There are any number of chapels, all splendid in one way or the other, set along the perimeter of St. Peter's basilica, to begin with the **Chapel of the Pietà**, named after Michelangelo's famous marble sculpture of the *Pietà* which the young artist made between 1499 and 1500 for cardinal Jean de Bilheres. After the **Chapel of Saint Sebastian** (which contains Francesco Messina's *Monument to Pope Pius XII)* is the better known **Chapel of the Holy Sacrament** with Bernini's *ciborium* mentioned above and the bronze railing designed by Borromini; next is the **Gregoriana Chapel**, a late 16th-century work

The Tomb of Saint Peter.

Michelangelo's Pietà.

finished by Giacomo della Porta and heavily decorated with *mosaics* and precious marbles; the **Chapel of the Column** with the astounding marble altarpiece depicting the *Encounter between St. Leo and Attila* by Algardi, and with the *sepulchers* of the many popes named Leo — the II, III, IV, XII; the **Clementina Chapel**, named after Pope Clement VII, built for him by Giacomo della Porta, which houses the mortal remains of St. Gregory the Great; and, also by Della Porta, the sumptuous **Chapel of the Choir** decorated with gilded stuccoes; finally the **Chapel of the Presentation** with the recent *Monument to Pope John XXIII*, by Emilio Greco.

The Basilica of St. Peter's in Vatican also contains a whole collection of famous monuments, from Michelangelo's *Pietà* to the venerated *effigy of St. Peter* shown in the act of blessing, which dates to the 13th century; Bernini's *Funeral Monument for Pope Urban VIII*, and the analogous *Funeral Complex for Paul III* by Guglielmo Della Porta, the *bronze Tomb* created by Antonio Pollaiolo for Pope Innocent VIII, which

was part of the original St. Peter's, and the neoclassic *Monument to the Stuarts* by Canova. Brief mention must also be made of the *baptismal font*, in porphyry, once part of a classical sarcophagus (and then used as the sepulcher for Otho II), transformed into a baptismal font by Carlo Fontana.

The imposing **Sacristy** lies before the left transept. Large as a church, it was conceived of as an independent building, and consists of the **Sagrestia Comune** on an octagonal central plan, the so-called **Sacristy of the Canons**, and the **Chapter Hall**. It was all designed by the Roman Carlo Marchionni at the behest of Pius VI, who laid the first stone in 1776.

Annexed to the Basilica is the **Museo della Fabbrica di San Pietro**, or Historical Artistic Museum, which includes the *Treasury of St. Peter's*. It was designed by Giovan Battista Giovenale and contains the remains of the enormous patrimony of the church which was repeatedly scattered and carried off by the Saracens, the Sack of Rome in 1527, the Napoleonic confiscations.

VATICAN PALACES

One of the most sumptuous and articulated monumental complexes in the world is without doubt that of the Vatican Palaces, which began to be built in the 14th century so as to house as befitted their rank the popes who had finally « returned » from their stay in Avignon, and who had previously resided in the Lateran. The first pope to take up permanent abode in the Vatican was Gregory XI and his successors later enlarged and beautified the complex. In 1410 Alexander V had the communication « corridor » built between the palace and Castel Sant'Angelo. But the greatest impetus to the building and organization of the sumptuous complex was provided by Nicholas V. The heart of the complex is the square palace which encloses the famous **Cortile del Pappagallo**, and on which Leon Battista Alberti and Bernardo Rossellino as well as others worked. The **Chapel of Nicholas V** is dedicated to Saints Stephen and Laurence and is decorated with *frescoes* by Fra Angelico.

The world-famous **Sistine Chapel** was created between 1473 and 1480, under Sixtus IV, when Giovanni de' Dolci reconstructed what was originally the Palatine Chapel. Innocent VIII even went so far as to have himself a **Palazzetto** built on the highest point of the Belvedere. The building appears in Andrea Mantegna's paintings, but was then lost with Bramante's reorganization and a still later construction of the Museo Pio Clementino under Pope Pius VI. When Alexander VI once more took up residence in the square **Palace of Nicholas V**, his enlargement was terminated by the erection of the **Borgia Tower** (named after the pope's family).

The maecenas pope, Julius II, sponsored a reorganization which could fall under the heading of town planning when he entrusted Bramante with finding the solution of how to connect the Palace of Nicholas V with that of Innocent VII: the result was, as is known, the **Courtyard of the Belvedere** with the *niche* by Pirro Ligorio (1560) at one end, in turn derived from the transformation of Bramante's exedra with its twin flight of stairs. Bramante was also responsible for the elevation of the **Loggias of the Courtyard of Saint Damasus**, finished and decorated with frescoes by Raphael. Thanks to this expansion, the Pope's Palace could now face out on Piazza San Pietro. Between 1509 and 1512 Michelangelo frescoed the vault of the Sistine Chapel for Julius II, and in 1508 Raphael began to decorate the Stanze, which were finished in 1524. After the disastrous sack of Rome, which to some extent brought the grand papal project of the *Instauratio Urbis* to a halt, work on the Vatican Palace continued under Paul III, who entrusted Antonio da Sangallo the Younger with the building of the **Cappella Paolina**, the **Sala Ducale**, and the

The statue of Laocoon in the Vatican Museums.

The Belvedere Apollo in the Octagonal Courtyard.

Sala Regia, entrusting the decoration of the Cappella Paolina and the termination of the frescoes in the Sistine to Michelangelo. The highlight of the Baroque in the Vatican Palace coincides with the papacy of Sixtus V and the architect Domenico Fontana, who designed the present papal residence and « cut » the Belvedere with the **Cortile trasversale** (now seat of the **Sistine Hall** of the Library).

In the 17th century, Urban VIII had the **Scala Regia** begun on designs by Bernini, as well as the **Pauline Rooms** in the Library and the Archives. In the following century the transformation into museums of part of the great complex was begun: the **Christian Museum** (**Museo Sacro**) and the **Profane Museum** (**Museo Profano**) (connected to the **Library**) were joined by the **Pio-Clementine Museum**, planned and installed by Michelangelo Simonetti and Giuseppe Camporese (1771-1793); by the **Chiaramonti Sculpture Gallery** bound to the name of Antonio Canova (1806-1810); the so-called **Braccio Nuovo** or **New Wing** designed by Raffaele Stern for Pius VII. Lastly, in the 20th century, Pope Pius XII initiated archaeological excavations under the Basilica of St. Peter's, while John XXIII turned his attention to the construction of new rooms which could better house the museum collections of the Lateran Palace.

Two rooms in the Vatican Museums with, below left, the Apostolic Library.

Disputation on the Holy Sacrament, by Raphael,
in the Stanza della Segnatura.

RAPHAEL'S STANZE

The rooms known as Raphael's Stanze because they contain so many of the painter's masterpieces, were built under the papacy of Nicholas V. Their decoration was initially entrusted to Andrea del Castagno, Benedetto Bonfigli and Piero della Francesca. Afterwards, under Julius II, the undertaking passed to Lorenzo Lotto, Perugino, Sodoma, Baldassarre Peruzzi, and Bramantino. Only in the last phase, upon Bramante's advice, did Julius call in Raphael, who was already famous. The painter was also flanked by a choice team of « advisors ». Chronologically the first Stanza to be frescoed, or rather the vault, was the **Stanza della Segnatura**, so-called because this

was where the court of the Segnatura met. Here Raphael painted the *Disputa* or *Disputation on the Sacrament*, which was thus his first pictorial work in Rome and which depicts the exaltation of the glory of the Eucharist rather than a « dispute ». Even more famous is the fresco on the wall across from the Disputa, the so-called *School of Athens*, which gathers the wise men and philosophers of antiquity together with the « contemporary » artists and lords, in other words the protagonists of the Renaissance, in an imposing architectural setting where they are all assembled around the great ancients, Plato and Aristotle. The composition of *Parnassus*, which decorates the wall of the window overlooking the Belvedere, is dated 1511 (the year is on the lintel of the window). The vault of the same Stanza has medallions which

*Expulsion of Heliodorus, by Raphael,
in the Stanza di Eliodoro.*

contain symbolic representations of *Philosophy, Justice, Poetry, Theology*, and panels with the *Fall of man, The Judgement of Solomon, Apollo and Marsyas, Astronomy*.

Next, chronologically speaking, is the **Stanza di Eliodoro**, which furnishes an example of what might be called historical painting, for Raphael had proposed various miraculous events which were decisive in the story of the Church, perhaps suggested by Julius II. These included *Leo I repulsing Attila*, the *Mass of Bolsena*, the *Expulsion of Heliodorus*, the *Liberation of St. Peter*. These date to the years 1512-1514, while the vault was presumably frescoed by De Marcillat, who most likely continued Raphael's ideas.

The decoration of the **Stanza dell'Incendio** however dates to 1514-1517. The name derives from the leading fresco which depicts the event of 847 when the *Fire in the Borgo* was miraculously stopped when Leo IV made the sign of the cross. An interesting detail in the fresco shows us the main facade of old St. Peter's, which had not yet been torn down when the picture was painted. The last of the Stanze is the **Sala di Costantino**, which cannot really be said to be by Raphael for the work was carried out almost entirely by Giulio Romano after the Master's death, although the plans were certainly his. It was finished in 1525. The decoration depicts episodes — famous and less famous — in the life of the emperor Constantine: from the *Baptism* (on the entrance wall), to the *Battle against Maxentius* (on the facing wall), the *Apparition of the Cross*, the mythical *Donation*. Raffaellino Del Colle and, above all, Francesco Penni were Giulio Romano's collaborators.

SISTINE CHAPEL

Between 1475 and 1481, under the pontificate of Sixtus IV Della Rovere, Giovannino de' Dolci, on a plan by Baccio Pontelli, built what may be called the Chapel of Chapels. Architecturally the Sistine Chapel is a spacious rectangular hall with a barrel vault, divided into two unequal parts by a splendid marble *transenna* or screen by Mino da Fiesole together with Giovanni il Dalmata and Andrea Bregno. The same artists also made the *choir loft*.

But the chief attractions of the Sistine Chapel are of course its frescoes, particularly those by Michelangelo, on the walls and vault. Michelangelo's marvelous paintings, however, came after others, which had been painted under the pontificate of Sixtus IV between 1481 and 1483, and which cover the wall facing the altar and the two side walls (these include paintings by Perugino, Pinturicchio, Luca Signorelli, Cosimo Rosselli, Domenico Ghirlandaio, Botticelli). The vault was blue and scattered with stars until Julius II commissioned Michelangelo to redecorate the vast surface.

Michelangelo worked on the ceiling from 1508 to 1512 and created a powerful architectural framework for the well known figures of the *Sibyls* and the *Prophets*, the elegant bold *Ignudi*, the nine *Stories from Genesis*, including the universally famous *Creation of Man*.

Twenty-five years later, between 1536 and 1541, Michelangelo returned to the Sistine Chapel, this time under the papacy of Paul III Farnese. The new great fresco of the *Last Judgement* covers the whole back wall of the Sistine Chapel and it was so large that two of Perugino's frescoes had to be destroyed and two large arched windows had to be walled up.

A view of the Sistine Chapel with Michelangelo's frescoes after restoration.

The Creation of Man by Michelangelo after restoration.

The Original Sin by Michelangelo after restoration.

MICHELANGELO IN THE SISTINE CHAPEL

Michelangelo, the famed master of the Sistine Chapel, completed his frescoes in two phases: the period between 1508 and 1512 was employed in painting the vaults under commission of Pope Julius II, whereas his other masterpiece, the Last Judgement, was commissioned by Pope Clement VII for the back wall of the chapel nearly a quarter of a century later. These two frescoes, which cover a surface of approximately 800 square meters, represent perhaps the greatest artistic achievement of all time. Beginning from the back, of the left-hand, side of the vault we can see: Jeremiah in meditation, *the* Persian Sibyl reading, Ezekiel holding a papyrus as he listens to an angel, *the* Eritrean Subyl consulting a book, Joel reading a papyrus, Zachariah consulting a book, *the* Delphic Sibyl unwinding a papyrus, Isiah in meditation with a book in his hand, *the* Cumaean Sibyl opening a book, Daniel writing, *the* Libyan Sibyl turning to pick up a book *and last* Jonah in ecstasy at the moment of his exit from the whale's belly.

Above these twelve figures, softly rendered nude figures support festoons and medallions. In the center, nine pictures reproduce the stories of the Genesis: beginning from the one above the altar we find: God separating light from darkness, God creating the Sun, the Moon, and the plants on Earth, God separating the waters and creating fish and birds, *followed by the well-known* Creation of Adam, *the* Creation of Eve from Adam's rib, *the* Original sin *and the* Expulsion of Adam and Eve from the garden of Eden, *the* Flood, *and* Noah's drunkenness. *The vault is also crowned by numerous triangular sections depicting other stories from the Old Testament:* Judith and Holofernes, David and Goliath, Ahasuerus, Esther and Haman, *and the* Bronze serpent. *The lunettes of the windows, and above them the vault sections, contain equally splendid frescoes depicting Christ's ancestors. An impressive pictorial composition representing the* Last Judgement *rotates around the commanding figures of Christ.*

THE RESTORED SISTINE CHAPEL

The restoration of Michelangelo's great frescoes on the vault of the Sistine Chapel and of the Last Judgement has finally been terminated. Merit goes above all to the contribution of the Nippon Television Network Corporation which employed sophisticated technological means in the television filming of each detail.

Begun in 1981 and shown to the public in the spring of 1994, the restored works took scholars by surprise and in part opened up new questions regarding the literature on the master's oeuvre which, up to that time had centered around Michelangelo's somber hues and his introspective approach to color. As the work of restoration progressed, layers of candle smoke, damage due to atmospheric agents and other causes were removed and the authentic colors gradually emerged. The frescoes can once more be seen in their original glowing light-toned hues, unquestionably more shocking and modern than those that preceded them.

A « rediscovered » Michelangelo, the painter of the Sistine Chapel, who continues to amaze us even after almost five centuries.

Next pages: the vault of the Sixtine Chapel after restoration.

A lunette restored.

Michelangelo's Moses between Rachel and Leah.

executors of the Pope's will is dated May 6, 1513, and stipulated for twenty-eight figures and three reliefs, all to be set in a suitable architectural setting. The entire project was to be finished in seven years at a total cost of 16,500 gold ducats. But as time went by, the project kept shrinking and the successive stages of the project are witnessed by contracts of 1516 and 1532. Ultimately the final agreement between the artist and the heirs provided for only three statues by Michelangelo and three by Raffaelo da Montelupo. All that now remains in San Pietro in Vincoli is the famous Moses, seated between *Rachel* (or the *Contemplative Life*) and *Leah* (or the *Active Life*), while the mortal remains of Julius II were wretchedly lost during the ill-omened sack of Rome in 1527. In the second half of the 16th century, still further modifications were carried out on the old Early Christian Basilica which had already been so heavily restored. An additional structure was added above the portico, which ended up by concealing the old openings so that new ones had to be put in. In 1705 Francesco Fontana, son of Carlo, was charged by Giovan Battista Pamphili with the screening off of the open trussed timber beams of the roof by means of a large wooden vault, while the framing of the portal on the interior by an aedicule dates to sixty years later. This was also when the Basilica was repaved in brick, altering the original level by raising the floor about ten centimeters. The last change was made by Vespignani and is mentioned here because it is an important element in the present aspect of the church. Vespignani worked on the area of the presbytery and replaced the Baroque altar with a typical open *ciborium* preceded by the confessio.

63

The facade and interior of San Giovanni in Laterano.

BASILICA OF SAN GIOVANNI IN LATERANO

Built by Constantine, plundered by the Vandals of Genseric, frequently sacked, damaged by the earthquake of 896 and various fires, the Basilica of St. John Lateran was continuously being rebuilt and restored, with the participation of Giovanni di Stefano, of Francesco Borromini, who brought it up to date for Innocent X, and Alessandro Galilei, who redid the facade in 1735. **Outside**, the Cathedral of Rome is characterized by the monumental architectonic structure of the giant Corinthian order used by Galilei, and it is enlivened by the jutting central part and the balustrade, above the attic, and the colossal statues of *Christ*, *Saints John the Baptist* and *John the Evangelist* and the *Doctors of the Church*. There are five entrances (the last to the right is known as « Porta Santa » and is opened only for the Holy Year or jubilee), surmounted by five loggias.

The imposing **interior** is a Latin cross with a nave and two aisles on either side. The antique columns were encased in robust piers, while grooved pilasters support a rich trabeation and above, a sumptuous ceiling, said to have been designed by Pirro Ligorio. Along the walls are ranged the figures of *Prophets*, *Saints*, and *Apostles* designed by Borromini but executed by his followers in the 18th century. At the crossing, the visitor unexpectedly finds himself at the Gothic heart of the Basilica: the *tabernacle* by Giovanni di Stefano, an airy slender silhouette against the gilded grates which enclose the precious relics of the heads of Saints Peter and Paul. Another of St. Peter's relics, the rough wooden altar table on which the apostle is said to have celebrated mass in the catacombs, is preserved in the papal altar. A double flight of stairs leads to the subterranean burial of Martin V, with its well-known *tomb slab* by Simone Ghini, probably under Donatello's supervision. The great conch of the apse at the back of the Basilica is covered with mosaics which date to different periods. Some are 4th century, some 6th and some 13th century (note in particular the figures of the *Apostles*, signed by Jacopo Torriti). Above the organ, the large 19th-century frescoes by Francesco Grandi depicting episodes, both ancient and modern, concerning the *Founding and construction of the Basilica*. The decoration which entirely covers the transept also deals with this subject (including the *Conversion of Constantine*) and was completely restored under the papacy of Clement VIII by the architect Giovanni della Porta and the painter known as Cavalier d'Arpino. Right under Cavalier d'Arpino's fresco of the *Ascension of Christ* is the *gable* in gilded bronze and supported by antique bronze columns which protects the *Altar of the Sacrament*, designed for Clement VIII by Pietro Paolo Olivieri and holding a precious *ciborium* like a small classic temple. Among the chapels which were built in various periods as further decoration for the Basilica, note should be taken of the so-called **Cappella del Coro**, by Girolamo Rainaldi (1570-1655); the **Cappella del Crocifisso**, which preserves a fragment of the presumed *Funeral Monument of Nicholas IV*, attributed to Adeodato di Cosma (13th century); the **Cappella Massimo**, by Giacomo della Porta; the **Cappella Torlonia**, unlike the precedent, splendidly in neo-Reinassance style by the architect Raimondi (1850); the **Cappella Corsini**, architecturally completely self sufficient, on a Greek-cross plan, by Alessandro Galilei for Clement XII. A corridor leads to the **Old Sacristy**, with the *Annunciation* by Venusti, and a *St. John the Evangelist* by Cavalier d'Arpino, and to the **New Sacristy**, with the 15th-century *Annunciation* of Tuscan school.

SCALA SANTA

The **Palazzo** owes its name to the fact that it was originally built to contain, or incorporate, the **Pope's Chapel** or *Sancta Sanctorum*. Pope Sixtus V commissioned the palace from the architect Domenico Fontana in 1585-1590. The Chapel was originally part of a building known as « Patriarchio » (7th-8th century), when it housed the papal court. The name **Scala Santa** derives from an erroneous identification of one of the staircases of the Patriarchio with a flight of stairs that was part of Pilate's *Praetorium* and which therefore would have been ascended by Christ when he was judged by Pilate. Nowadays the *Sancta Sanctorum* is used to indicate the **Chapel of Saint Laurence**, overflowing with relics and at the same time a true jewel of Cosmatesque art.

The Scala Santa.

BASILICA OF SAN PAOLO FUORI LE MURA

Built by Constantine on the tomb of the apostle Paul, the church remained standing until July 15, 1823, when it was gutted by fire, not to be reconsecrated until 1854. On the **exterior**, St. Paul's now has an imposing quadriporticus in front of the main facade (on the side towards the Tiber) with 146 granite columns which define a space that is dominated by the statue of the *Apostle Paul*, by Pietro Canonica. The facade, which rises over the quadriporticus is richly decorated with mosaics both in the gable (the *Blessing Christ between Saints Peter and Paul*) and in the frieze (an *Agnus Dei* on a hill that rises up symbolically between the two holy cities of Jerusalem and Bethlehem) and the four large *Symbols of the Prophets*, which alternate with the three windows of the facade. The **interior** is just as richly decorated and is divided into a nave with two aisles on either side, separated by eighty columns in granite from Baveno. A continuous frieze runs along the crossing and the aisles with *Portraits of the 263 popes successors of Saint Peter*. On the walls, Corinthian pilasters rhythmically alternate with large windows with alabaster panes (which replace those destroyed in the explosion of 1893). The coffered ceiling has large gilded panels which stand out against the white ground.

Two imposing statues of *Saints Peter and Paul* overlook the

The facade of San Paolo fuori le Mura and the interior of the basilica.

raised transept with the sumptuous *triumphal arch*, called the *Arch of Galla Placidia*, which dates to the time of Leo the Great, framing the apse which was already decorated with mosaics in the 5th century. In the 13th century the mosaics were renewed by Honorius III, using Venetian craftsmen who were sent for the purpose to the pope by the doge of Venice. The mosaics depict a *Blessing Christ between Saints Peter, Paul, Andrew, and Luke*, while Honorius, significantly in much smaller proportions, kisses the foot of the Savior. The *Redeemer* is also set on the gold-ground mosaic in the triumphal arch, this time flanked by two *Adoring Angels* and the *Symbols of the Evangelists*, dominating the two rows of the *Elders of the Apocalypse* with the slightly off-center figures of *Saint Peter and Saint Paul* on either side on a blue ground. Objects housed in the Basilica include the *tabernacle* Arnolfo di Cambio made in 1285 in collaboration with a certain « Petro », identified by some as Pietro Cavallini, also thought to have executed the *mosaics* (of which only fragments remain) decorating the back side of the arch of triumph and which once adorned the exterior of the Basilica. Under the fine canopy of Arnolfo's tabernacle is the altar beneath which is the *tomb of Saint Paul* with the inevitable *fenestrella confessionis* (confessional window) through which can be seen the epigraph incised on the stone « Paulo Apostolo Mart. », dating to the 4th century.

Two sections of the elegant cloister of San Paolo fuori le Mura.

The Baths of Caracalla.

The statue of St. Sebastian (top) in the catacombs bearing the same, and the statue of St. Cecilia (bottom) in the catacombs of San Callisto.

BATHS OF CARACALLA

The Baths of Caracalla are the most imposing and best preserved example of thermae from the Imperial period still extant. They were built by Caracalla beginning in A.D. 212. In the 16th century excavations carried out in the enormous building brought to light various works of art including the *Farnese Bull* and the *Hercules*, now in the National Museum of Naples. *Mosaics with athletes*, which decorated the hemicycles of the large side courtyards of the thermae, were discovered in 1824 (Vatican Museums).

In their ground plan the Baths of Caracalla clearly distinguished between the actual bath sector and the surroundings where all the accessory non-bathing services were located. At present the central building is accessible and the itinerary is quite like that followed in antiquity by the bathers. The vestibule leads on the right into a square chamber, flanked by two small rooms on either side, covered with barrel vaults. This was the *apodyterium* (dressing-room). Next came one of the two large palaestrae from where the bathing itinerary generally started after various sports and exercises had been done in the palaestra. From here one went to a *laconicum* (turkish bath), the imposing *calidarium* (hot bath) and the *tepidarium* (temperate bath), a more modest rectangular chamber flanked by two pools. Next came the large central hall, the *frigidarium*. The *natatio*, which could also be reached from the *frigidarium*, was uncovered. It has a fine front elevation with groups of niches between columns, once meant to contain statues.

CATACOMBS

These deep galleries were once quarries for travertine and pozzolana. Situated at the periphery of Rome, they became meeting places for the early Christians and shortly thereafter were also used as cemeteries (1st-4th cent.). Mention will be made of those of Domitilla, Saint Calixtus, Saint Sebastian, Saint Agnes and Priscilla. In the 16th century they were rediscovered and reappraised after centuries of abandon.

The **Catacombs of Saint Domitilla**, known also as catacombs of SS. Achilleus and Nereus, are the largest in Rome and traditionally developed from a simple family burial ground that belonged to Domitilla, wife or niece of the consul Flavius Clemente put to death by Domitian. The catacombs contain the remains of the *Basilica of SS. Nereus and Achilleus*, behind the apse of which is a cubicle with the fresco of the *Deceased Veneranda invoking St. Petronilla*. The ancient burial grounds of the Aurelian Flavians lie near the basilica. In another part of the catacombs, named after the *Good Shepherd* because the earliest representation of this subject was found here, paintings from the 2nd century are to be found in the vault. Lastly, in the area of later date there are fine depictions of the grain market, scenes of daily life and work (3rd-4th cent.).

The **Catacombs of Saint Calixtus** are just as famous and extend for twenty kilometers. They were developed by Pope Calixtus III and became the official burial grounds for the bishops of Rome. They are excavated on four levels and contain the *Crypt of the Popes*, in which several of the early

IN MEMORY OF EDITH CECILIA McBRIDE OF NEW YORK U.S.A.

popes were buried. They contain interesting decorations as well as epigraphs of Pontianus Lucius Eutychianus and Sixtus II. The *Cubiculum of Saint Cecilia*, where the remains of this Christian martyr were found, is decorated with painting from the 7th and and 8th centuries. After this comes the *Gallery of the Sepulchers*, again with interesting paintings, the fine *Crypt of Pope Eusebius* and the *Crypt of Lucina*. The most remote parts of the necropolis (2nd cent. A.D.) are decorated with paintings of fish and symbols of the Eucharist.

The **Catacombs of Saint Sebastian** are also excavated on four levels: the first has been partially destroyed but still has an austere chapel where St. Philip Neri used to go to pray; on the second floor is an intimate crypt, known as the *Crypt of Saint Sebastian*, with a *Bust of the saint* attributed to Bernini. An underground passage leads to three tombs with decorations and stuccoes dating to the 1st century A.D.

The Palazzo della Civiltà del Lavoro in the quarter of EUR.

EUR

This famous district, at one and the same time the most recent and the most historical, was originally created for the Esposizione Universale di Rome (World Fair of Rome) to be held in 1942. Designed by a group of famous architects (Pagano, Piccinato, Vietti, and Rossi) coordinated and directed by Marcello Piacentini, it covers an area of 420 hectares in the shape of a pentagon.

The formative concept was that of monumentality and it was built with a view to the future expansion of Rome towards the Tyrrhenian Sea. Included among its significant paradigms of Italian architecture of the first half of the 20th century are the **Palazzo della Civiltà del Lavoro**, as well as the sites of the **Museo Preistorico ed Etnografico Pigorini**, the **Museo dell'Alto Medioevo (Early Middle Ages)**, the **Museo delle Arti e Tradizioni Popolari** and the **Museo della Civiltà Romana**.

TIVOLI

VILLA D'ESTE

Right outside Rome, Tivoli, the ancient *Tibur*, was already a favorite holiday resort for the Romans as well as a place for the worship of local divinities. It is now the site of the **Villa Gregoriana**, a fine **Cathedral**, the renowned **Rocca Pia**, and, above all, the **Villa d'Este**, with an Italian garden deservedly famous for its magic atmosphere.

Built on the ruins of a Roman villa, it was first a Benedictine convent and then the Governor's Palace, and as such was magnificently restored by Pirro Ligorio on commission of the governor at the time, Ippolito d'Este, around 1550. After various vicissitudes it became the property of Austria, was returned to the Italians in 1918, then restored before the monumental part and the immense park were opened to the public. Of note on the grounds is the **Loggia** by Pirro Ligorio, which is the finest part of the main facade which faces the city and the mountains.

The **Italian gardens**, with their geometric compartmentalization, the five hundred fountains, the age and rarity of the trees, is certainly one of the finest gardens to be found both in and outside Italy. No visit is complete without a stop at the *Grotto of Diana*, richly stuccoed with mythological scenes, the so-called « Rometta » or little Rome, with reproductions in an allusive key of parts of the city (the Isola Tiberina, the ruins), the various *Fountains of Bacchus*, the *Organ Fountain* (the water organ was designed by Claudio Vernard), the *fountains of Proserpine, of the Dragons* (signed by Ligorio), *of the « Mete », of the Eagles*, and so on, up to the romantic *Cypress Rotonda*, considered one of the most enchanting elements in both garden and villa. Even in this end of the garden signs of antiquity are present, as witnessed by the ruins of a **Roman villa** to the right of the Cypress Rotonda.

HADRIAN'S VILLA

Tivoli is also the site of an imposing architectural complex dating to Hadrian's time. This emperor's gifts as an architect can be seen in the series of palaces, baths, theaters, etc. which he had built there between 118 and 134, and which were meant to remind him, here in Italy, of the places he most loved in Greece and the Near East.

Mentioned for the first time in literature by Flavio Biondo, the Villa, or rather what was left of it, was visited and studied by famous persons (Pope Pius II, Pirro Ligorio) and excavations were carried out particularly in the 18th century (Piranesi made engravings of some parts). Bought by the Italian government in 1870 from the Braschi family which had owned it since the beginning of the 19th century, the villa was restored, while many of the works of art (especially sculpture) from the site can now be seen in the rooms of the Museo Nazionale Romano.

Mention will be made only of some of the best known and important places in the complex. For an idea of the entire set-up (and as orientation) a study of the model at the entrance, even though it is more a matter of hypothesis, can be useful. The monuments include the **Stoà Poikile** (commonly called Pecile) and the **Naval Theater**, the **Small Thermae** and the **Great Thermae**, the **Canopus** (with obvious reference to the sanctuary in Egypt), the **Museum** (with the precious objects found in the excavations, including a copy of the *Amazon* by Phidias), and lastly the **Emperor's Palace** subdivided into three blocks and aptly described as a « city in the shape of a palace ».

Villa d'Este in Tivoli.

A section of the Canopus on the grounds of Hadrian's Villa in Tivoli.

FLORENCE

The river Arno cuts its way through the broad plain on which Florence lies, surrounded by the out-hills of the Tusco-Emilian Apennines. Already occupied in prehistoric times, as early as the 8th century B.C. an Italic peoples with a Villanovan culture settled in the area between the Arno and Mugnone rivers, but little is known of these remote times. In 59 B.C. the Roman city was founded with the square ground plan of the castrum. The decumanus maximus was laid out along what are now the Via del Corso, the Via degli Speziali and the Via Strozzi, while the ancient cardo corresponds to the line between Piazza San Giovanni, the Via Roma and the Via Calimala. With the arrival of the barbarians, Florence was first besieged by the Ostrogoths (405) of Radagaisus, who plundered the surrounding countryside, although Florence managed to resist and Stilicho's troops inflicted an overwhelming defeat on the enemy. Next came the Byzantines, who occupied Florence in 539, and the Goths who took over the city in 541. Under Lombard domination (570) it managed to safeguard its autonomy, while under the Franks the number of inhabitants diminished and the city lost most of its territory. Around the year thousand, things began to change for the better and the «lily» city's rise continued for various centuries in spite of numerous controversies, wars and internecine struggles. New walls surrounded the city, new civic and religious buildings went up, and at the same time the arts, literature, and trade continued to prosper. In 1183 the city became a free commune, even though it had already actually availed itself of this freedom for many years. The first clashes between the two factions, Guelph and Ghibelline, date to those years. The former were followers of the Pope, the latter of the Emperor. The ensuing struggles were to lacerate the civic fabric of the city up to 1268. Despite the unstable social and political situation, this period witnessed an upsurge in the arts and in literature. This was the time of Dante and the «dolce stil novo», of Giotto and Arnolfo di Cambio. In the 15th century the city's rise continued. Florence was a trading city but also the new cradle for Italian and eventually European culture. Many powerful families (the Pitti, Frescobaldi, Strozzi, Albizi) vied for supremacy in the city. One above all soon came to the fore, a powerful family of bankers — the Medici — and beginning with the founder Cosimo I, later known as the Elder, they were to govern up to the first half of the 18th century, transforming Florence into a beacon during the period of Humanism and the Renaissance. Great personalities such as Leonardo da Vinci and Michelangelo characterized the period and Florentine prestige reached its zenith.

In 1737 the Medicis gave way to the house of Lorraine and the government continued along the lines of a moderate liberalism even if at that point the great period of Florentine culture was on the wane. In 1860, during the Risorgimento, Tuscany was annexed to the Realm of Italy with a plebiscite. For a brief period Florence then became the capital of the new nation.

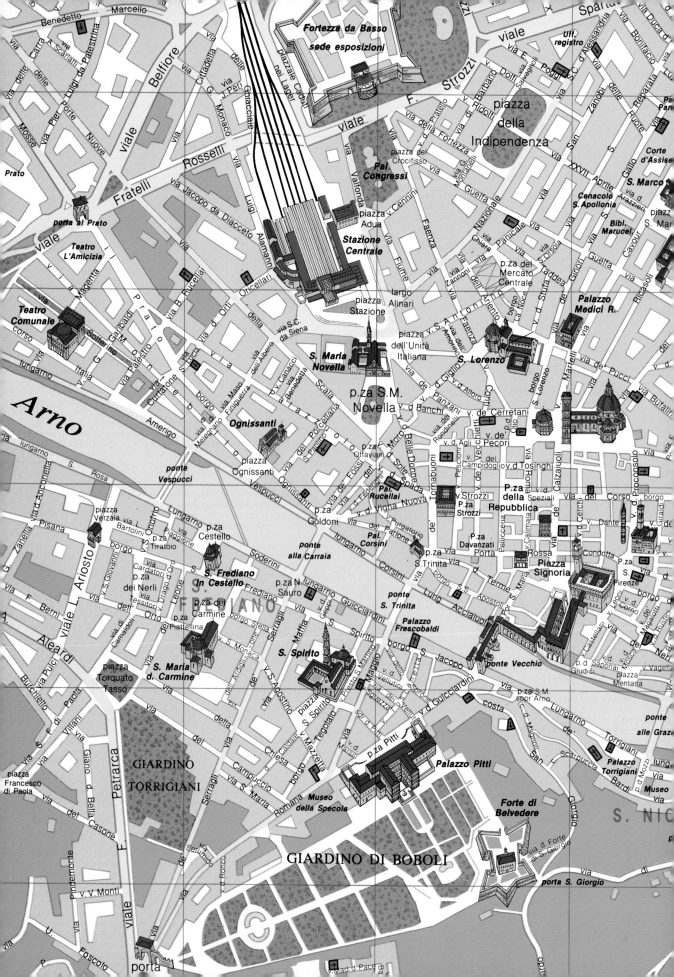

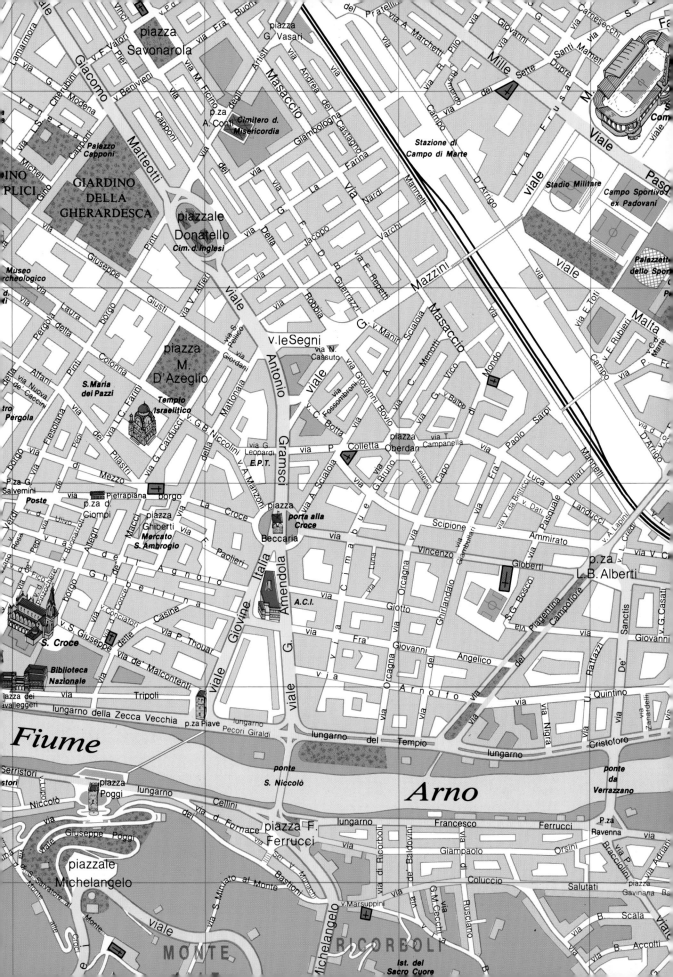

A view of the complex of the Duomo.

THE CATHEDRAL

DUOMO

Dedicated to S. Maria del Fiore, the Cathedral is the fruit of the dedicated work of the many artists who collaborated in its building for various centuries. In 1294 the Corporation of the Guilds commissioned Arnolfo di Cambio with the realization of a new Cathedral that was to replace the extant church of Santa Reparata. The cathedral workshop grew up around and inside the church, which continued to be used for decades, until 1375. Work on the new Cathedral or Duomo began on Sept. 8, 1296 and continued under various *capomastri* or directors of works such as Giotto, Andrea Pisano, Francesco Talenti, until 1375, when Santa Reparata was torn down and part of Arnolfo's project was altered. The dome had to wait until 1420, the year in which Brunelleschi won the competition for the building of this enormous structure. In 1434

work was terminated and two years later the church was consecrated, 140 years after it had been begun. The lantern was started in 1445 and finished in 1461 with the gilded sphere. Arnolfo di Cambio's unfinished **facade** of the Duomo was torn down in 1587. From then on, for almost three centuries, there was a continuous flow of projects and competitions for the new facade of the Cathedral until finally in 1871 the design presented by the architect Emilio de Fabris was approved (work ended in 1887). The facade — in the 19th-century Gothic style — betrays the historical point of view which ruled the taste of the times and employed the same types of marble previously used in the rest of the building - Carrara white, Prato green and Maremma pink. Above the three portals with *Stories of Mary* are three lunettes with, from left to right, *Charity*, the *Madonna with the Patron Saints of the City*, and *Faith*, the pediment over the central portal has a *Madon-*

The interior of the Duomo of Florence.

The bust of Filippo Brunelleschi.

na in Glory. The statues of the *Apostles* and of *Mary* are set in the frieze that runs between the rose windows at the sides and the one in the center. Above, after a series of busts of artists, is the pediment with the low relief of *God the Father*. The **Dome** is Brunelleschi's masterpiece, planned and raised between 1420 and 1434, put the finishing touch on the building of the Duomo. The great artist proposed to build the enormous airy dome without the use of fixed centering, thanks to the employment of ribbing with tie beams and bricks set in herringbone patterns, a double shell for the dome with an ogive form (at the drum the dome is 45.52 m. in diameter and 91 m. high) on a tall drum. The interior of the dome, which Brunelleschi envisioned bare, was frescoed by Vasari and Zuccari (1572-1579). In the 19th century, and recently, proposals have been made to restore the dome to its original pristine whiteness. The **lantern** was also designed by Brunelleschi and is in the form of a temple, raising the total height of the church to 107 meters.

In line with the dictates of Italian Gothic architecture there is a strong feeling for vertical and horizontal space **inside** the Duomo (the fourth largest church in the world: 153 meters long, 38 meters wide across the nave and aisles, and 90 at the transept). In the nave and aisles, piers with pilaster strips sup-

QVI COELVM CECINIT MEDIVMQVE IMVMQVE TRIBVNAL.   LVSTRAVITQVE ANIMO CVNCTA POETA SVO   DOCTVS ADEST DANTES SVA QVEM FLORENTIA SAEPE
SENSIT CONSILIIS AC PIETATE PATREM   NIL POTVIT TANTO MORS SAEVA NOCERE POETAE   QVEM VIVVM VIRTVS CARMEN IMAGO FACIT

*The panel by Domenico di Michelino with Dante
and the Divine Comedy.*

*A stretch of the walls of the old Cathedral of Santa Reparata
in the subterraneans of the Duomo.*

port large moderately pointed arches and ribbed Gothic
vaulting. A gallery on corbels runs along on high. At the back
is the high altar (by Baccio Bandinelli) surrounded by three
apses or **tribunes**, each subdivided into five rooms. The polychrome marble pavement (1526-1660) is by Baccio and
Giuliano d'Agnolo, Francesco da Sangallo and others. The
two equestrian monuments (frescoes transferred from the
wall) of *John Hawkwood* (Giovanni Acuto) and *Niccolo da
Tolentino* are on the wall of the left aisle. The former, of
1436, is by Paolo Uccello; the latter, of 1456, by Andrea del
Castagno (note the diversity in the modelling of the figures of
these two mercenary captains: severity as opposed to vitality).
To be noted among the many other works are the *Tomb of
Antonio d'Orso* by Tino di Camaino (1321); the lunette with
the *Crowned Madonna* by Gaddo Gaddi; and in the left aisle
the tabernacle with *Joshua* by Ciuffagni, Donatello and Nanni
di Bartolo; the *Bust of Squarcialupi* by da Maiano, the panels
with *Saints Cosmas and Damian* by Bicci di Lorenzo.

SANTA REPARATA

The old cathedral of Florence was originally built in the 4th-
5th centuries on the ruins of a Roman domus, with columns
dividing the nave from the two side aisles and a single apse.

During the Byzantine wars the church was destroyed, to be rebuilt between the 7th and 9th centuries. The perimeter remained almost the same but the building was enriched by two side chapels and the columns were replaced by piers with engaged pilasters. Between the year 1000 and 1100 a crypt was added under the apse and the choir was raised, while two bell towers were built near the apse. When the new Cathedral of Santa Maria del Fiore was built, this ancient church, dedicated to the young saint who died a martyr in Caesarea, had to relinquish its site. The new Cathedral however was built around the old church which was not torn down until its completion in 1375. In 1966 when the pavement of the Duomo had to be restored, remains of the preceding cathedral came to light. Now an entrance situated between the first and second piers of the right aisle of the Duomo leads down into a spacious chamber where thanks to the structures installed by the architect Morozzi, the remains of *frescoes* which once decorated the church, the *tombstones* of various prelates and civil authorities (as well as the slab which indicates *Brunelleschi's tomb*), and stretches of the brick and mosaic pavements can still be seen.

GIOTTO'S CAMPANILE

The Cathedral bell tower was begun in 1334 by Giotto, who as *capomastro* was overseer for the construction of the Duomo.

Up to his death in 1337, he built the bottom part of the campanile comprised of two closed stages decorated with hexagonal and rhomboid *reliefs*, by Andrea Pisano, Luca della Robbia, Alberto Arnoldi and workshop. The relief panels on the lower band, now replaced by casts, represent the *Life of Man with Genesis* and *Arts and Industries executed* by Andrea Pisano and Luca della Robbia to Giotto's designs.

The two upper stages were carried to completion by Andrea Pisano, who took Giotto's place at the time. He created a series of sixteen niches between the pilaster strips which contained statues of the *Prophets*, *Sibyls* and the *Baptist* (the originals are to be found in the Museo dell'Opera del Duomo), surmounted by an equal number of false niches. Between 1350 and 1359 Francesco Talenti finished the campanile, adding two levels with the two gabled two-light windows with their lovely twisted columns and the stage with the single three-light opening.

The Campanile by Giotto.

BAPTISTERY

This octagonal building with semicircular apses, raised on a stepped podium, was originally built in the 4th-5th centuries near the north gate of Roman Florence. Its current appearance dates to the 11th-13th centuries: the smooth pyramidal roof was terminated in 1128, the **lantern** with columns dates to 1150, the rectangular **tribune** (the « scarsella ») to 1202. The exterior is faced with green and white marble. Each side is divided into three sections by pilaster strips surmounted by trabeation and round arches with windows. Particularly striking are the bronze doors and, inside, the mosaics in the dome. There are three sets of doors in the Baptistery of San Giovanni: the **south doors** by Andrea Pisano with *Stories of the life of the Baptist* and *Allegories of the Virtues*, the **north doors** by Ghiberti, with *Stories from the New Testament, Evangelists* and *Doctors of the Church*, and the **east doors** (or **Gates of Paradise**), Ghiberti's masterpiece and deservedly the most famous of the three. They are divided into ten panels which depict *Stories from the Old Testament* and were commissioned by the Arte dei Mercanti in 1425. In the perfection of execution, they are worthy of the name Michelangelo bestowed on them. Small figures of biblical personages and *portraits of contemporary artists* are to be found in the frame around the panels.

Two views of the Baptistery of San Giovanni.

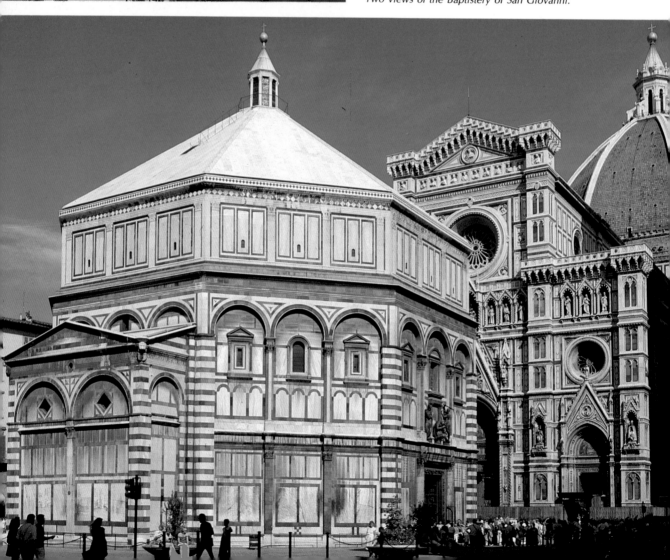

Interior of the Baptistery.

The Tomb of the Anti-Pope John XXIII designed by Michelozzo and Donatello.

Next page:
the octagon of the cupola completely lined with mosaic decoration.

The **interior** of the Baptistery is characterized by the walls on two orders, the inferior one with columns and the upper one with pillars between mullioned windows. The surfaces are covered by marble geometrical tarsias similar to those of the floor. Particularly interesting the *tomb of the Antipope John XXIII*, a complex built by Michelozzo and Donatello (the latter made the reclining statue), two *Roman sarcofagi* and the tomb *slab of Bishop Ranieri*. The **apse** is enriched by beautiful *mosaics* of the thirteenth century, coeval to those of the large dome. Next to the large *Enthroned Christ* by Coppo di Marcovaldo, six tiers of bands representing, from the base to the top, *scenes from the life of Saint John the Baptist, stories of Christ, of Joseph, of Genesis, Celestial Hierarchies* and ornamental motifs.

PALAZZO VECCHIO

Begun in 1294 and intended as a palace-fortress for the residence of the Priors, Arnolfo di Cambio conceived of the building as a large squared block terminated by a row of crenellations. It is characterized by the powerful thrust of the *Tower* of 1310 (94 m. high) which rises from the Gallery. Externally the structure is in rusticated ashlars of *pietra forte* which lend the large building, divided into three floors and decorated with two-light openings inscribed in round-headed arches, a highly impressive air and a sense of austerity. Between 1343 and 1592 modifications and additions were made to Arnolfo's original nucleus, both inside and out (Cronaca, Vasari, Buontalenti all worked on it). The mechanism of the *clock* dates to 1667.

Various statues are lined up in front of the Palazzo Vecchio, including a copy of Michelangelo's *David*, that replaced the original in 1873, and the group of *Hercules and Cacus* by Bandinelli. On the **facade**, above the door, there is a medallion with the monogram of Christ between two lions in a blue field, surmounted by a gable. The inscription « *Rex regum et Dominus dominantium* », was placed there in 1551 by order of Cosimo I.

After passing through **Michelozzo's Court**, with gilded stucco columns and frescoes by Vasari, and with Verrocchio's *Fountain with a Winged Putto holding a Fish* in the center, Vasari's broad staircase leads to the imposing **Salone dei Cinquecento**, and to the **Studiolo of Francesco I**, created by Vasari and full of *panels* painted by Bronzino, Santi di Tito, Stradano, as well as bronze statues by Giambologna and Ammannati. Access to the **State Apartments** is also from the Salone dei Cinquecento. The numerous rooms full of paintings and frescoes include the **Hall of Leo X** (at present occupied by the Mayor and the City Councilors); the **Hall of Clement VII** with Vasari's famous fresco of the *Siege of Florence* with a detailed view of the 16th-century city; the **Hall of Giovanni dalle Bande Nere**, the **Halls of Cosimo the Elder, Lorenzo the Magnificent** and of **Cosimo I**.

SALONE DEI CINQUECENTO

The Salone dei Cinquecento (prepared to house the assemblies of the Consiglio Generale del Popolo after the Medicis had been expelled from Florence for the second time) is by Cronaca, while the frescoes were entrusted to Vasari. The allegorical paintings on the ceiling and the walls narrate the triumphal *Return of Grand Duke Cosimo I to Florence*, illustrate the possessions of the *Medici Ducato* and the *Stories of the Conquest of Pisa and Siena*. The marble statues include, on the right hand wall, Michelangelo's striking *Genius of Victory*.

The interior of the asymmetrical Salone dei Cinquecento, richly decorated with painting and sculpture.

PALAZZO DEL BARGELLO

The Palazzo del Bargello is like a fortress with powerful embattlements (the **Volognana**). It was built in 1255 as the seat of the Capitano del Popolo, and the Podestà and the Consiglio di Giustizia were then housed there. In 1574 it became the living quarters for the Bargello (Captain of Justice, or chief of police). The interior is centered around a **courtyard** with porticoes on three sides. A picturesque **covered staircase**, built in the 14th century by Neri di Fioravante, leads to the upper **loggia**, by Tone di Giovanni (1319). Since 1859 the place has been the site of the **Museo Nazionale** (one of the most important in the world) which contains Renaissance sculpture and masterpieces of the minor arts from varying periods.

MUSEO NAZIONALE DEL BARGELLO

The enormous **Entrance hall** on piers with solid vaulting has heraldic decorations on the walls with the coats of arms of the podesta (13th-14th cent.). From here to the scenographic **Courtyard** which is irregular and unique. The coats of arms of many podesta are here and, under the portico, the picturesque insignia of the quarters and the districts into which the city was once divided. Various 16th-century *statues* set against the walls are by Bandinelli, Ammannati, Giambologna and Danti.

The courtyard leads to a **Hall** with a collection of 14th-century sculpture, including Tino da Camaino's *Madonna and Child with Angel*, a meditating *Madonna and Child* of Venetian school, the *base of a holy water stoup* by Nicola Pisano and a *Madonna between St. Peter and St. Paul* by Paolo di Giovanni (circa 1328). In the Room close to the open staircase are important works by Michelangelo: the *Bacchus* (1470), an early work of great power despite the softness of form, the *Pitti Tondo*, with the Madonna teaching Jesus and

The Bargello with the tower of the Volognana.

The portico in the courtyard of the Bargello.

Bacchus by Sansovino.

Bacchus by Michelangelo.

The model for Cellini's Perseus.

St. John to read (1504), the *David or Apollo (1530), the Brutus* (1540). There are also works by Ammannati, Giambologna (including his famous Mercury of 1564) Tribolo, Danti, Francavilla and Sansovino who made a *Bacchus* of his own to compete with Michelangelo's. The bronze *bust of Cosimo I* by Cellini made for Portoferraio in Elba and brought back in 1781, is also in the same room.

The **Open Staircase**, leads to the **Loggia**, ornamented with various works by other 16th-century artists.

The first room to the right, once the Salone del Consiglio Generale, is now the **Donatello Room** and contains many of his works such as the *St. George* (1416) with its self-contained energy, made for the niche in Orsanmichele the young *St. John*, slender and mystical, the marble *David* (1408) and the bronze *David*, the first delicate Renaissance nude made around 1430. Also by Donatello are the *Marzocco*, the symbol of the city, and the lively bronze *Amor-Attis*, revealing a classic influence. In addition to works by Luca della Robbia, Ghiberti, Vecchietta and Agostino di Duccio, the room also contains the *trial panels* which Ghiberti and Brunelleschi made in 1402 for the competition (there were six contestants) for the second doors of the Florentine Baptistery.

Access to the **Collection of Decorative Arts**, mostly based on the donation of the Carrand Collections, is from the hall. *Goldwork* and *enamels* from the Middle Ages to the 16th century, *seals* and various metal objects are in the **Salone del Podestà**. In the adjacent **Cappella del Podestà**, where those condemned to death passed their last hours, there are Giottesque frescoes with *Paradise, Hell* and *Stories of the Saints*. The floor is completed by the **Sala degli Avori**, with rare carvings from the ancient period to the 15th century; the **Sala delle Oreficerie**, with numerous works of sacred art, and the **Sala delle Majoliche**.

The second floor of the Bargello contains other rooms dedicated to great artists: the first, known as the **Giovanni della Robbia Room**, contains a number of the master's sculptures including the predella with *Christ* and *Saints, St. Dominic*, the *Pietà* and the *Annunciation*.

The following **Andrea della Robbia Room** houses the *Madonna degli Architetti* and other works in glazed terracotta. In the **Verrocchio Room** are the *Resurrection*, the *bust of a young woman*, the *Madonna and Child*, the bronze *David* and other works by the master as well as various *busts* and *sculpture* by Mino da Fiesole and the group of *Hercules and Antaeus* by Pollaiolo, with the vibrating force of the two struggling figures. Other bronze sculpture is in the **Sala dei Bronzetti** with the *mantelpiece of Casa Borgherini* by Benedetto da Rovezzano; the **Sala delle Armi** houses military paraphernalia from the Middle Ages to the 17th century. The museum is completed by the **Sala della Torre** with tapestries and the **Medagliere Mediceo** with works by artists such as Pisanello, Cellini, Michelozzo and others.

A view of Santa Croce.

CHURCH OF SANTA CROCE

This monument is truly unique, not only for the purity of the Gothic style, but also for the famous works of art it contains and its historical importance. The Basilica of Santa Croce, one of the largest churches in the city, is attributed to the genius of Arnolfo di Cambio who seems to have begun work in 1294. Work continued into the second half of the 14th century but the church was not consecrated until 1443. The facade with its three gables dates to the 19th century (project by N. Matas) and the **campanile** in Gothic style also dates to this period (1847, project by G. Baccani). A portico of airy arches runs along the left flank and shelters the 14th-century *tomb of Francesco Pazzi*. On the right side of the church are the **Cloisters**, with the **Pazzi Chapel** in the background, and the **Museo dell'Opera di S. Croce**. The imposing interior has a nave and two side aisles separated by slender octagonal piers from which spring spacious pointed arches with a double molding. The beauty of the Church has been partially obfuscated by 16th-century remodelling. The floor is covered with old tombstones for the entire length of the nave which has a trussed timber ceiling. The transept has a number of chapels, including the **Cappella Maggiore** with the *Legend of the Holy Cross* (1380) by Agnolo Gaddi. On the altar is Geri-

ni's polyptych with the *Madonna and Saints* and, above, the *Crucifix* of the school of Giotto. A *Deposition from the Cross* (cartoon by Lorenzo Ghiberti) in stained glass can be admired on the interior facade. Below to the right is the *Monument to Gino Capponi* (1876), and to the left that to *G. B. Niccolini* (1883). A splendid marble *pulpit* by Benedetto da Maiano (1472-76) stands in the nave. To be noted in the right aisle, at the first altar, is a *Crucifixion* by Santi di Tito (1579); on the first pier is the famous bas-relief by Antonio Rossellino (1478) of the *Madonna del Latte*. The *stained-glass windows* date to the 14th century. The most famous *funeral monuments* are along the walls of the right aisle. These include the monument to *Dante Alighieri* by Ricci (1829); to *Michelangelo*, by Vasari (1579); to *Alfieri*, by Canova (1803); to *Machiavelli*, by I. Spinazzi (1787). Fragments of *frescoes* by Orcagna are to be seen behind the fourth altar and further on is Domenico Veneziano's fine fresco (1450) of *St. John the Baptist and St. Francis*. Next comes the tabernacle in *pietra serena* by Donatello and Michelozzo with the *Annunciation* (1435 c.) by Donatello. and then the *Tomb of Leonardo Bruni* by Bernardo Rossellino, the *funeral monument to Rossini* and the one to Foscolo. The right arm of the transept contains the **Castellani Chapel** superbly frescoed by Agnolo Gaddi (1385) with *Stories of the Saints*. On the altar a *Crucifix* by Gerini.

At the end of the transept is the **Baroncelli Chapel**, with the splendid Gothic *tomb* of the Baroncelli family and a lunette with a *Madonna* by Taddeo Gaddi. The frescoes on the walls with *Stories of Mary* are also by Gaddi and the *Madonna of the Girdle* is by Bastiano Mainardi (1490). The *Coronation of the Virgin* on the altar is by Giotto. Michelozzo's portal leads to the **Sacristy**, with the **Rinuccini Chapel** frescoed with *Stories of the Magdalen and the Virgin* by Giovanni da Milano. The fine *altarpiece* is by Giovanni del Biondo (1379). Michelozzo's **Medici Chapel**, built for Cosimo the Elder, is at the back. It contains a magnificent *bas-relief* by Donatello and various works by the Della Robbias. Various chapels (14th-cent.) with important works open off the central zone of the transept. These include the **Velluti Chapel** with *Stories of St. Michael Archangel*, perhaps by Cimabue; the **Chapels of the Peruzzi and the Bardi** families frescoed by Giotto with *Stories of St. John the Evangelist* (1320) and *Stories of St. Francis* (1318); the **Tosinghi Chapel** with the *Assumption in Heaven*, also by Giotto; the **Pulci Chapel** with frescoes by Bernardo Daddi. Of particular note in the left aisle is the *Marsuppini Sepulcher* by Desiderio da Settignano.

PAZZI CHAPEL

At the back of the Basilica's **First Cloister** is the **Pazzi Chapel**, a daring example of Brunelleschi's genius begun in 1443. The decorations are by Desiderio da Settignano, Luca della Robbia, Giuliano da Maiano. The **Museo dell'Opera di S. Croce** has been installed in the **Refectory**, to the right of the **Cloister**.

The Cappella Maggiore, in Santa Croce.

The side of the Uffizi overlooking the Arno.

UFFIZI

The gallery of the Uffizi is the most famous picture gallery in Italy and one of the best known in the world. It furnishes a complete panorama of the various schools of Florentine painting, represented by important works and authentic masterpieces. It also includes numerous collections of other Italian schools (particularly the Venetian) and a fine group of Flemish paintings, as well as the famous collections of self-portraits. To be noted also are the antique statues and an extensive collection of tapestries. The Uffizi was commissioned from Giorgio Vasari by the Medicis as administrative and judicial offices (thence the name). Begun in 1560 and finished twenty years later, the two wings with a loggiato at the bottom are connected by a third wing with arches along the Arno. On either side of the central courtyard powerful piers

contain niches with 19th-century statues of illustrious Tuscans, while the upper floors of the building have windows (1st floor) and a running loggia (2nd floor). In addition to the **Gallery**, which is on the second floor, the building houses the **State Archives** which contain rare documents from the city's history. On the ground floor note should be taken of the remains of the Romanesque church of **San Piero in Scheraggio** (brought to light and restored in 1971) with fine frescoes by Andrea del Castagno. On the first floor is the **Gabinetto dei Disegni e delle Stampe** (Drawing and Print Cabinet), an imposing collection begun in the 17th century at the behest of Cardinal Leopoldo de' Medici.

The visit to the Gallery begins on the second floor. This great museum did not become public patrimony until 1737, a gift of Anna Maria Ludovica de' Medici, the last of this prestigious family. The gallery consists of 45 rooms divided into sections.

Santa Trinita Madonna by Cimabue.

Ognissanti Madonna by Giotto.

The panel with Christ the Redeemer and four Saints by Meliore di Jacopo.
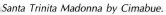

Annunciation by Leonardo da Vinci.

*The Duke and Duchess of Urbino
by Piero della Francesca.*

Madonna and Child with Saints by Ghirlandaio.

Adoration of the Shepherds by Lorenzo di Credi.

95

Magnificat Madonna by Botticelli.

Primavera and Birth of Venus by Botticelli.

Holy Family (Doni Tondo) by Michelangelo.

Venus and Cupid by Alessandro Allori;
below: Henriette of France as Flora
by Jean Marc Nattier.

◀ *Ponte Vecchio on the downstream side of the Arno.*

◀ *A detail of some of the workshops on the bridge and the arches which support Vasari's Corridor.*

Ponte Santa Trinita and Ponte Vecchio.

BRIDGES OF FLORENCE AND THE PONTE VECCHIO

Currently there are ten Florentine bridges, but until 1957 there were six, modified in the course of the centuries and all, except the Ponte Vecchio, rebuilt after their destruction in 1944 by mines. The **Ponte Vecchio** is the oldest bridge in the city, not only because it is the only one which survived, but also because it stands on the site of at least three precedent bridges: one in Roman times, the one that was ruined in 1117, and the one destroyed when the Arno flooded in 1333. The bridge so greatly admired now was built by Neri di Fioravante (1345), a solid but elegant structure with three arches. It is characterized by the small houses that line both sides of the bridge. In the 14th century these rows of buildings had a much more regular appearance but as time went by various changes and additions led to their current picturesque variety. At about the center of the span over the river, the buildings are interrupted by a widening of the roadway, thus furnishing a fine view of the Arno and the other bridges.

Vasari's Corridor passes along over the bridge, above the buildings. It allowed Cosimo I to reach Palazzo Pitti from Palazzo Vecchio without running any risks. Ever since the 16th century the shops on the bridge have been the laboratory-shops of goldsmiths (previously some of them were butcher shops). The second Florentine bridge was the **Ponte Nuovo** or **Ponte alla Carraia** (1220), which served for the heavy traffic of the time. It was also reconstructed after the floc of 1274 and 1333, and then once more after it fell in 1944. The third bridge was the **Ponte alle Grazie** (1237), so-called because of a chapel dedicated to the Madonna delle Grazie. What we see now is post-war. The fourth bridge is the **Ponte S. Trinita**, a masterpiece by Ammannati (1567-70); Michelangelo supervised the project. It replaced previous bridges (the earliest dated to 1257) which had been carried away by the floods. At the beginning and end of the bridge are the statues of the *Four Seasons* (set there in 1608). The present bridge is the result of a reconstruction carried out « as it was and where it was » in the 1950s, after it had been destroyed in the war. The other two bridges date to the 19th century-the one of **S. Niccolò** and the one at the Cascine (which was originally a suspended bridge), rebaptized in 1928 **Ponte alla Vittoria**. The **Ponte Vespucci** was inaugurated in 1957. It is the first modern bridge and the seventh in the series. In 1969 **Ponte Giovanni da Verrazzano** was added and, recently, the **Viaduct of the Indian**, beyond the Cascine, and the one of **Varlungo**.

CHURCH OF ORSANMICHELE

Once a loggia used as a grain market (built by Arnolfo di Cambio, 1290), it was destroyed in a fire in 1304. Rebuilt in 1337 (the work of Francesco Talenti, Neri di Fioravante and Neri di Cione), between 1380 and 1404 the structure was transformed into a church. The austere lines of the large cubic building (with the arcading serving as a base) are softened by the late Gothic marble decoration. The upper part is in *pietra forte* with two tiers of large twolight openings. Niches and tabernacles with statues are set into the outer walls (particularly famous are Ghiberti's *St. John the Baptist*, 1414-16; Verrocchio's *St Thomas*, 1464-83; Nanni di Banco's *Four Crowned Martyrs*, 1408; the copy of Donatello's *St. George*, 1416). Inside the church is the imposing *Tabernacle* by Orcagna, in flamboyant Gothic style (1355-59).

Church of Orsanmichele: Orcagna's tabernacle and the interior of the church.

The facade of Santa Maria Novella and one of the obelisks in the piazza.

CHURCH OF SANTA MARIA NOVELLA

The Dominican friars, Sisto da Firenze and Ristoro da Campi, began to build the church in 1246 on the site of the 10th-century Dominican oratory of S. Maria delle Vigne. The nave and aisles went up in 1279 and the building was finished in the middle of the 14th century with the **campanile** and the **Sacristy** by Jacopo Talenti.

The marvelous facade was remodelled between 1456 and 1470 by Leon Battista Alberti (the original facade was early 14th century) who created the splendid portal and everything above it, articulated in inlaid squares and bordered by the *heraldic sails* of the Rucellai family who commissioned the work. Two large reversed volutes tie the lateral masses together with those in the center, articulated by four engaged pilasters and terminating in a triangular pediment. The interior is divided into a nave and two aisles by compound piers with pointed arches, and 16th-century renovation.

The church houses in its **interior** numerous works from the 14th to the 16th centuries. Of particular note are the *Monument to the Beata Villana* by Rossellino (1451); the *Bust of St. Antoninus* (in terra cotta) and the *Tomb of the Bishop of Fiesole* by Tino da Camaino; Ghiberti's lovely *tombstone for Leonardo Dati* (1423); the *Tomb of Filippo Strozzi* by Benedetto da Maiano 1491); Vasari's *Madonna of the Rosary* (1568); the *Miracle of Jesus* by Bronzino. Be sure to stop for a while in the **Cappella Maggiore** (or *Tornabuoni Chapel*), with a fine bronze *Crucifx* by Giambologna on the altar and frescoes with the *Stories of St. John the Baptist* and *Stories of*

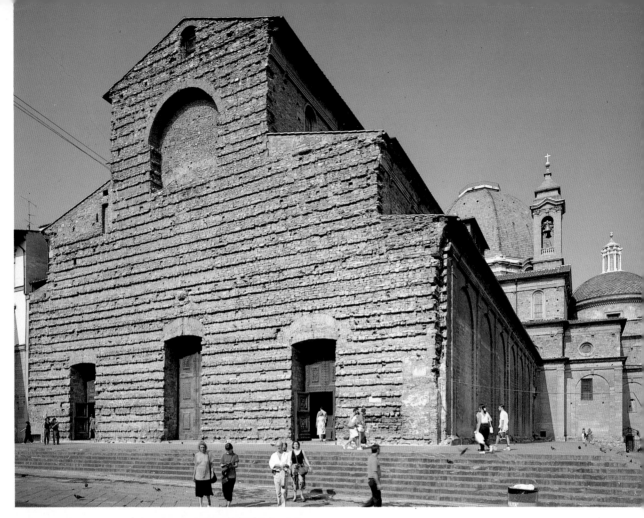

The facade of the Church of San Lorenzo and the Cloister.

the *Madonna* by Domenico Ghirlandaio, late 15th cent.), the **Gondi Chapel**, by Giuliano da Sangallo, with fragments of *frescoes* by 13th-century Greek painters on the vault and Brunelleschi's famous *Crucifix* on the back wall; the **Cappella Strozzi di Mantova**, with frescoes of the *Last Judgement* on the back wall, *Hell* on the right wall and *Paradise* on the left, by Nardo di Cione or Orcagna. The gate to the left of the facade leads to the **First Cloister**, in Romanesque style (1350) frescoed with *Scenes from the Old Testament* by Paolo Uccello (now in the **Refectory**). From here, through the **Chiostrino dei Morti**, one arrives at the **Chiostro Grande**, with more than fifty arches and completely lined with frescoes by Florentine masters of the 15th and 16th centuries.

CHURCH OF SAN LORENZO

This is the oldest church in the city (consecrated by St. Ambrose in 393) and it was rebuilt along Romanesque lines in 1060. What we see now is Brunelleschi's adaptation of 1423. The facade, magnificent and moving in its bareness, was supposed to be faced with marble (Michelangelo's project was never carried out). Of particular note inside, among others, are Donatello's two *bronze pulpits and his choir-loft*, as well as the **Old Sacristy**, Brunelleschi's first work (1419-28).

MEDICI CHAPELS

The large complex, containing the tombs of the Medici, is just behind the Church of San Lorenzo. Various rooms aru the vault are in common. From the entrance vestibule we enter a vast, low room, created by Buontalenti, where we can find the *tombs of Donatello, Cosimo the Elder members of the Lorraine dynasty* as well as other grand-ducal tombs. The staircase leads to the large **Chapel of the Princes**, created and begun by Nigetti (with additional touches by Buontalenti) in 1602; it was finished in the eighteenth century. The interior is octagonal in shape, completely clad in pietradura and marble in line with the Baroque taste; above the base with *16 coats-of-arms* of th grand-ducal cities, there are *6 sarcophagi* of the grand dukes *Cosimo III, Francesco I, Cosimo I, Ferdinando I, Cosimo II, Ferdinando II*, two of which have statues of the *Grand Dukes* by Tacca. A corridor leads from the Chapel of the Princes to the **New Sacristy**.

The Chapel of the Princes.

The tomb of Lorenzo, duke of Urbino: Dawn, by Michelangelo.

The head of Michelangelo's David.

Michelangelo's sculpture in the Tribune of the Accademia.

GALLERIA DELL'ACCADEMIA

The Gallery houses an extremely important collection of sculpture by Michelangelo. The room that leads to the tribune, hung with tapestries, contains the *Palestrina Pietà*, whose attribution to Michelangelo is controversial, the unfinished *St. Matthew*, made for the Florentine cathedral, and the four « *Prisons* » (or slaves) which were meant for the tomb of Julius II in St. Peter's in Rome, which was never finished, like these male figures who seem to be trying to free themselves from the marble grip. At the center of the spacious **Tribune** is the original of the *David* (1501-4) commissioned from the great sculptor to replace Donatello's *Judith* on the balustrade of the Palazzo dei Priori. The room also contains an important collection of *paintings* of the Tuscan school of the 13th and 14th centuries. **Three small rooms** are to the right of the *Tribune* and contain various *shrines* attributed to Bernardo Daddi and a fine *Pietà* by Giovanni da Milano. To the left another series of **three small rooms** which contain works by famous masters of the 14th century: of note are a fine *Polyptych* by Andrea Orcagna, and two series of panels representing *Scenes from the Life of Christ* and *Scenes from the Life of St. Francis*, by Taddeo Gaddi. To the left of the Tribune there is another large **hall** containing works of the Florentine 15th century, including Lorenzo Monaco's *Annunciation*, Filippino Lippi's *St. John the Baptist and the Magdalen*, the *Madonna of the Sea*, attributed either ta Botticelli or Filippino Lippi, and a fine *panel from a wedding chest*, known as the *Adimari wedding chest*, by an unknown Florentine painter of the 15th century.

The room in the Galleria dell'Accademia with the Rape of the Sabines by Giambologna.

The Assumption and Saints by Perugino (Galleria dell'Accademia).

CONVENT AND CHURCH OF SAN MARCO

The **Convent** already existed in the 12th century. In 1437 Cosimo the Elder commissioned Michelozzo with the restructuration and it therefore became the first Florentine convent structure to be built in elegant essential Renaissance form. The lovely **Cloister** has simple element in stone with brick cornices; on the ground floor the space is enclosed by airy arcades. On the first floor there are fine *lunettes* frescoed by Poccetti, Rosselli, Coccapani, Vanni, Cerrini, Dandini and other illustrious artists. The main entrance to the convent lies to the right of the **Church of San Marco**. This too was restored in 1437 by Michelozzo. It was later renovated by Giambologna (1580) and then by Silvani (1678). The simple facade was redone between 1777 and 1780 by Gioacchino Pronti. The linear interior has an outstanding carved and gilded *ceiling*. Of interest is the **Sacristy**, and the adjacent **Chapel of St. Antoninus**, decorated by Giambologna, Francavilla. Alessandro Allori; the frescoes in the dome are by Poccetti. But the true center of attraction of this religious complex is without doubt the Convent. It is well known that an exceptional artist, Fra Angelico, lived and worked within these ancient walls. Most of the frescoes in the **Cloister** (particularly beautiful are the *Crucifix with St. Dominic* at the entrance and the lunette over the door with *St. Peter Martyr*) are his. He also painted the St. *Dominic* in the **Chapter Hall** and a splendid *Crucifixion* inside; a *Pietà* over the door of the **Refectory**; *Jesus as a Pilgrim* over the **Hospice** door, and inside, the *Madonna dell'Arte dei Linaioli*, the *Last Judgement*, the *Stories of Jesus*, the *Deposition*. Through the **Refectory**, stairs lead to the upper floor, where Fra Angelico's *Annunciation* is most striking. The corridor leads to Michelozzo's **Library** and, at the end of the corridor, to **Cosimo's Cell** with a *Crucifix* by Angelico in the antecell and the *Adoration of the Magi* in the cell. In the corridor to the left is the *Madonna Enthroned with Saints*, and then other splendid works by Fra Angelico are to be found in the cells which open off the corridor; the *Annunciation*, the *Transfiguration*, *Jesus before the Praetor*, the *Maries at the Sepulcher*, the *Coronation*, the *Presentation in the Temple*. At the end of the corridor is **Savonarola's Cell** (the *Portrait of the martyr* is by Fra Bartolomeo). A staircase to the right leads into the **Small Refectory** with a large fresco of the *Last Supper* by Domenico Ghirlandaio (a version of the more famous one in Ognissanti).

The Cloister of S. Marco.

Crucifixion by Fra Angelico.

A panoramic view of Florence from Piazzale Michelangelo.

*The group of bronze figures cast
from Michelangelo's works.*

The Forte di Belvedere.

PIAZZALE MICHELANGELO

Piazzale Michelangelo is approached from the **Viale dei Colli** that winds its way up the southern slope of Florence for about six kilometers. Both were designed by the architect Giuseppe Poggi in 1868. The Piazzale, a wide terrace overlooking Florence, is centered by a group of bronze figures cast from the original sculptures by Michelangelo (*David* and the four *allegorical statues* that decorate the Medici tombs in the New Sacresty of San Lorenzo).

THE FORTE DI BELVEDERE

Designed by Bernardo Buontalenti (1590-95), the fort was built at the order of Ferdinando I de' Medici on a hilltop dominating Florence for strategic military purposes. It has been restored recently and is used now for important international exhibitions. It offers one of the best views of Florence.

The facade of the Church of San Miniato al Monte.

The interior of the church

CHURCH OF SAN MINIATO AL MONTE

Bishop Hildebrand had the present structure built in 1018 on the site of a 4th-century chapel. The lower part of the facade is decorated by fine arcading; the upper part is simpler and has a fine 12th-century mosaic of *Christ between the Madonna and St. Miniato*. The church, with its unfinished **15th-century campanile** that was damaged during the siege of Florence in 1530, the **Bishop's Palace**, the **fortifications**, the **monumental cemetery** all stand at the top of a hill called Monte alle Croci, which rises up over the Piazzale Michelangelo below and over the entire city. The **interior** of this magnificent example of Florentine Romanesque architecture (it originally belonged to the Benedictine monks and then passed to the Olivetan friars in 1373) is tripartite with a trussed timber roof.

Outstanding is the pavement in the center with marble intarsias of signs of the *zodiac* and *symbolic animals*. The walls retain fragments of 13th- and 14th-century *frescoes*. Of note is the **crypt**, a vast space closed off by an elaborate wrought-iron gate (1338). The *altar* (11th-cent.) preserves the bones of St. Miniato. Fragments of *frescoes* by Taddeo Gaddi (1341) can be seen in the vaults of the crypt. The raised **presbytery** is of great beauty with its *pulpit* (1207) and a *choir* with fine inlaid wooden choir stalls. The large mosaic of the *Blessing Christ flanked by the Madonna and Saints* (1297) is in the conch of the apse. Entrance to the **Sacristy**, completely frescoed by Spinello Aretino (1387) with the sixteen *Stories of the legend of St. Benedict*, is to the right of the presbytery. On the left, stairs lead to the **Chapel of St. James**, or « of the Cardinal of Portugal », designed by Antonio Manetti and decorated with five roundels representing the *Holy Spirit* and the *Cardinal Virtues*, by Luca della Robbia (1461-66). To the right is the *funeral monument of the Cardinal*, a particularly lovely work by Antonio Rossellino (1461). The **Chapel of the Crucifix** designed by Michelozzo, and with delicate glazed vaulting by Luca della Robbia, stands at the center of the church. To the right of the church is the **Bishop's Palace** (1295-1320), ancient summer residence of the bishops of Florence which then became a convent, a hospital and a Jesuit house.

112

Palazzo Pitti and the Piazza.

The Bacchus Fountain in the Boboli Gardens.

PALAZZO PITTI

The most imposing of the Florentine palaces dates to 1457 and was probably designed by Brunelleschi. Ammannati enlarged it in the 16th century. The facade (205 m. long and 36 m. high) is covered by a powerful rustication in enormous blocks of stone. The only decorative element are the crowned lion heads set between the window corbels on the ground floor. The two projecting wings date to the period of the Lorrainers. The large arched portal leads through an atrium into Ammannati's **courtyard** which lies lower than the hill of Boboli. The **Royal apartments** and the **Palatine Gallery** are on the first floor on the second is the **Gallery of Modern Art**. The palace also contains the **Museo degli Argenti** and the **Museo delle Carrozze**.

BOBOLI GARDENS

These gardens comprise the largest monumental green area in Florence. Their history goes back over four centuries, for Cosimo I commissioned the designs from Niccolò Pericoli, known as Tribolo, in 1549. Work was continued by Ammannati, Buontalenti and Parigi the Younger. Noteworthy places are: **Buontalenti's Grotto** (1583), the **Amphitheater** with the *Roman basin* and the *Egyptian obelisk* at the center; **Neptune's Fishpond;** the statue of *Plenty* by Giambologna and Tacca (1563); the **Grand Duke's Casino**, the **Cavalier's Garden**; Parigi's **Fountain of the Ocean** (1618).

Raphael's Madonna of the Chair in the Palatine Gallery.

PALATINE GALLERY

The Palatine Gallery, which is the second museum for extension and importance after the Uffizi contains works of enormous value for the history of art. It was realized by Ferdinando II de' Medici with decoration by Pietro da Cortona. The works are placed according to a sixteenth century conception; the pictures are in fact displayed on the walls in an essentially decorative way.

The collection was enriched by Cardinal Lorenzo de' Medici, by the last members of the Medici family, and by the Lorrainers. The Gallery is formed of many rooms dedicated to gods and mythological characters depicted in the decorations.

CENACOLO OF GHIRLANDAIO

One of Ghirlandaio's masterpieces is to be seen in the **Refectory** of the **Church of Ognissanti** (built in 1256 but thoroughly remodelled in the 17th cent.), after passing through Michelozzo's **Cloister**. This painting of the *Last Supper* (1480) is characterized by the new approach in describing the poses of the Apostles and the use of a landscape (delicate and serene) behind them. These elements may have influenced Leonardo da Vinci who saw the painting two years before leaving Florence.

CHURCH OF SAN FREDIANO IN CESTELLO

The Church of S. Frediano in Cestello, even though the facade was never finished, is a rare example of the Baroque in Florence. It was built by Antonio Maria Ferri (on a design by the Roman Cerutti), 1680-89. The **cupola** on a drum (1698) is also his. Inside, the fine *fresco* in the cupola is by Gabbiani (1701-1718). The church is probably called Cestello because of the vicinity of Cosimo III's Granary, which stands on the eastern side of the square.

CHURCH OF SANTO SPIRITO

S. Spirito was meant by Brunelleschi to be a twin to S. Lorenzo, but the facade was never finished. The **dome** too is by Brunelleschi while the **campanile** is by Baccio d'Agnolo (1503). The interior is one of the finest examples of Renaissance architecture.

The Church of Ognissanti and Ghirlandaio's Last Supper in the Refectory adjacent to the church.

The Church of San Frediano in Cestello, and, below, the Church of S. Spirito.

CHURCH OF THE CARMINE

The 14th-century church of S. Maria del Carmine was almost completely destroyed in a fire in 1771. The **Brancacci Chapel** in the right transept contains a fresco cycle painted between 1425 and 1428 by Masolino and above all, by Masaccio (the *Temptation* is by the former, the famous *Expulsion from Paradise* and a series of scenes from the *Life of St. Peter*, including the well-known *Tribute Money*, are by the latter). The frescoes were finished by Filippino Lippi.

BRANCACCI CHAPEL: THE RESTORATION

The chapel preserves the most exalting cycle of frescoes known to western art, thanks to the presence of as extraordinary a painter as Masaccio who worked there from 1425 to 1427, in collaboration with Masolino, and the fact that it was finished more than 50 years later by Filippino Lippi. Recent restoration (1984-88) has eliminated retouching and overpainting of the past which had turned the colors into a heavy monochrome, and has restored the frescoes to what they originally were, where form, color and brilliance are marvellously balanced, as is evident in these two details taken from Masaccio's *Tribute Money* and Masolino's *Resurrection of Tabitha*.

The facade of the Church of the Carmine.

The nave of the Church, and, right, the frescoed dome.

Views of the frescoes in the Brancacci Chapel, once more to be seen in their original splendor thanks to recent meticulous restoration.

The Church of San Francesco.

The Roman Theater.

View of the two knolls of Fiesole.

Piazza Mino da Fiesole.

FIESOLE

This ancient Etruscan city, standing on its hill, dominates Florence. The center consists of the beautiful **Piazza Mino da Fiesole** where the **Cathedral of S. Romolo** is situated. The Church, founded in the 11th century, contains the *Salutati Chapel*, with frescoes of the 15th century by Cosimo Rosselli and the *tomb of Bishop Salutati*, by Mino da Fiesole. The **Bishop's Palace** (11th cent.) and the old **Church of S. Maria Primerana** lie across from the Cathedral. Not far off is the **Church** and the **Convent of S. Francesco** (14th cent.), which houses the **Ethnographic Museum of Missions** with important Etruscan finds. The **Archaeological Civic Museum** and the wonderful **Roman Theater**, dated to the 1st century B.C., can be rapidly reached from the square. Nowadays the theater is usually used for numerous theatrical and cinematographical events. Nearby are the **Roman Baths** and the **Etrusco-Roman Temple**. The **Bandini Museum** with its sculptures and paintings from the 13th to the 15th century and the old **Basilica S. Alessandro** must not be overlooked.

VENICE

Water-girt Venice rises on an archipelago of small islands separated by a dense network of waterways, which were rectified as time passed, noticeably changing the original conformation. Venice lies four kilometers from the mainland and two from the open sea.

The original inhabited nucleus of the city took shape during the barbarian invasions when groups of refugees from Spina, Aquileia, Adria, Altino, Padua settled on the islands in the lagoon. In the course of the centuries the population kept increasing, developing into a city the likes of which is not to be found anywhere in the world. It must also be kept in mind that since over 160 waterways have been covered with earth, the number of islands on which Venice stands has been reduced to eighteen, inclusive of San Giorgio Maggiore and the Giudecca.

The longest of the canals (3.8 km.) and the widest (from 30 to 70 m.) is the Grand Canal which divides the city into two parts that are interconnected by three bridges: the Bridge of the Scalzi, the Bridge of Rialto and that of the Accademia. Forty-five rii or internal canals run into the Grand Canal and they can all be navigated with small boats or gondolas. As many as 350 bridges connect the various zones of the city. The territory is subdivided into sestrieri or districts: Cannaregio, San Marco, Castello, Dorsoduro, San Polo, Santa Croce. Until 1480 the bridges were in wood; later they were replaced by arched stone structures.

Land travel moves over spaces that have their own specific names.

There are not many main streets, rughe (from the French rue) and the salizade or first streets in the city to be paved (sel-ciate). The smaller alleys are called cale or calle while those that run close to the canals and serve as foundations for the houses are known as fondamenta; the lista is that stretch of road next to an ambassadorial residence which enjoyed a particular diplomatic immunity. In addition there are the mercerie, streets lined by shops of various kinds, the rive which are stretches of fondamenta along the rii, the smaller waterways, and more specifically the steps which lead to the water from the fondamenta. Rii terà are filled-in canals, the rami are short stretches of road that branch off from a calle or a campiello. The campo is the square near a church, a large area of open ground once cultivated, mostly as a vegetable garden or used to pasture horses. The campiello is the smaller open space between the houses, to which the calli lead. The small open areas surrounded by buildings and with only one entrance/exit are known as corti. Paludo is the name given to those spaces where there was once a swamp (palude) while the pissine are on the sites of pools where it was possible to fish and swim.

Basically Venice today still looks as it did in the 13th century, with the exception of a few transformations in various buildings which however play an unimportant part in the general layout of the city plan.

Insular Venice covers an area of a little over seven square kilometers, inclusive of the islands of San Giorgio and the Giudecca. The area that falls under the jurisdiction of the Commune of Venice is much larger, comprising other important inhabited centers: the islands of Murano, Burano and Torcello, inside the lagoon, the Lido and Pellestrina towards the sea, Malcontenta, Dese, Tessera, Mestre and Marghera, Zelarino, Carpenedo, Asseggiano, Trivignano, Favaro and Chirignago in the immediate hinterland. Some of these places were once autonomous communes.

Dogana da Mar.

The Church of Santa Maria della Salute.

DOGANA DA MAR

The complex of the Maritime Customs House, at the far end of the sestiere (district) of Dorsoduro, is a sort of spearhead jutting out into the lagoon and dividing the Grand Canal from the Canal of the Giudecca. Behind it, beyond the Seminary, Santa Maria della Salute looms up.

CHURCH OF SANTA MARIA DELLA SALUTE

In 1630 with the plague raging in Venice, the Senate made a vow to erect a church to the Madonna when the scourge came to an end. In fulfillment of this obligation Baldassarre Longhena designed Santa Maria della Salute, which was consecrated in 1687, five years after the architect's death. The church is unquestionably one of the great monuments of the Venetian Baroque.

The building is octagonal in plan with arches dominated by a dome on a drum and with six side chapels. A flight of stairs leads to the **facade** which looks like a rich triumphal arch, with chapels set into the sides of the octagon. The first three altars on the right in the **interior** have paintings by Luca Giordano and the third altar on the left has a late work by Titian of the *Pentecost*. Around 1674 Giusto Le Court created the marble group on the high altar, meant to house the Holy Image that was venerated in San Tito in Candia and then brought to Venice in 1672 when the Turks occupied the city. The sculpture shows us the *Plague fleeing from the Madonna*. Originally the commission was to have been given to Bernini, but he refused. Canvases by Titian are in the ceiling of the **large Sacristy** and the tabernacle has a fine mosaic in pietre dure of the Byzantine school of the 12th century. The Venetians flock to the church in pilgrimage on the 21st of November, the day dedicated to the Madonna della Salute.

A view of Piazza San Marco.

PIAZZA SAN MARCO

A gem among gems in the field of Italian architecture the Piazza San Marco consists of two large contiguous areas: the Piazza itself and its extension, the Piazzetta, which runs down to the sea. Unrivalled examples of architecture face out on this large open space on all sides: the **Basilica of San Marco**, the **Palace of the Doges** or Palazzo Ducale, the **Loggetta**, the tall **Clock Tower**.

The original layout of the Piazza dates to the 9th cent. A.D., and it is essentially still the same despite the various changes that have been made throughout the centuries. As early as the second half of the 12th century Doge Sebastiano Ziani modified the piazza, doubling the space in front of the Basilica, and setting up the two large monolithic columns which ideally close off the Piazzetta. A century later both the Basilica and the Palace of the Doges were variously transformed, and the

fortified ducal residence became the elegant building with loggias that we see today. At the time, the Piazza was surrounded by interesting buildings such as the headquarters of the Canons of San Marco, the houses of the Procurators, and the Church of San Geminiano, with numerous shops facing out on the Piazzetta. The real transformation of the Piazza began in 1400: many buildings were torn down, the Clock Tower (late 15th cent.) was built, and the Zecca or Mint and the Library were constructed, joined a hundred years later by the Procuratie Nuove. In Sansovino's new project for the Piazza the underlying basic structures followed the original arrangement. At the beginning of the 1700s the centuries-old red brick pavement with its herringbone design was replaced with the grey trachite stone from the Euganean Hills which thousands of visitors still tread under foot today.

CAMPANILE OF SAN MARCO

The Piazza San Marco is dominated by the lofty bell tower about 100 meters high called « *el paron de casa* » (the master of the house) by the Venetians. But it did not always look like this. In the 9th century, a lookout tower stood on the site which at the time faced directly onto the lagoon since the Piazzetta San Marco (now between the Libreria Marciana and the Palace of the Doges) was a sort of inner harbor. Rebuilt in the second half of the 12th century, two sides of the campanile were at the time set against the buildings which stood in front of the present Procuratie Nuove (the Ospizio Orseolo) and in the area of the Libreria, constituting the corner.

Frequently damaged, it was rebuilt between 1511 and 1514 by Bartolomeo Bon on a project by Giorgio Spavento. Set apart from the adjacent buildings, the shaft of the powerful stocky tower has pilasters up to the arches which make it look like a pier of the classic period. Over the belfry, pierced by four-light openings, is a drum which supports the pyramidal steeple and the statue of the *Archangel Gabriel*. Inaugurated with great pomp, the structure stood intact until 1902, when it suddenly crumbled. It was decided to rebuild it « *com'era e dov'era* » (as it was and where it was). Reconstruction terminated in 1912, including Sansovino's Loggetta which had been gravely damaged when the bell tower fell. Nowadays, from the belfry where Galileo tried out his telescope, a magnificent panorama can be had over the lagoon and the city as far as the Alps.

CLOCK TOWER

The Clock Tower, built by Codussi between 1496 and 1499, is undoubtedly one of the most photographed monuments in Venice, thanks both to the presence of the original clock and to the two « *Moors* » who strike the hours at the top of the tower. The construction of the lateral parts, designed by P. Lombardo, was begun in 1506 and they were raised higher in 1775 by Giorgio Massari. The bronze « *Moors* » by Ambrogio da le Anchore date to 1497.

Below the Moors is the Lion of San Marco. On the small semicircular terrace further down is a gilt copper statue of the *Madonna and Child* by A. Leopardi and during Ascension week three statues move across the terrace from left to right, passing before the Virgin. The large clock is a masterpiece of clockwork mechanism by Giampaolo and Giancarlo Ranieri from Parma (late 15th cent.), indicating the passing of the seasons, the phases of the moon and the movement of the sun from one sign of the zodiac to the other.

The Campanile of San Marco.

the interior and two facades on the exterior, was built to provide access to all the offices of the various magistrates. An inscription by Vittoria on the loggia at the top of the Giants' Staircase refers to the visit the King of France, Henri III, made to Venice in 1574. Under the inscription is one of the many « lion's mouths » into which secret denunciations were inserted. The doorway to the right of the inscription leads to the **Hall of the lower Chancellory**, office of the « segretario alle voci » whose task it was to keep the registers of the offices and the proclamations for the elections. Then comes the **Stanza dei Provveditori alla Milizia da Mar**, a magistrature instituted in 1571 charged with raising an armed navy capable of defeating the Turks. As time passed their field of competence grew, eventually including the exacting of the « tithe », a tax of 10% on the wages of those in the pay of the Republic as well as of private individuals.

The **First Room** and the **Second Room of the Avogaria** were the offices of the Avogadori de Comun, fiscal lawyers comparable to a district attorney. They were also entrusted with the « Libro d'Oro » (Book of Gold) and the « Libro d'Argento » (Book of Silver), respectively listing the nobility and the bourgeoisie. Through a corridor it was possible to go from the second hall to the **Bridge of Sighs**, and from there to the **Prisons** which had two sections: the « piombi » and the « pozzi ». The latter (the wells) were situated at the level of the lagoon and were for those who had committed more serious crimes.

The **Scala d'Oro** or Golden Staircase, begun in 1583 on a design by Sansovino and completed by Scarpagnino in 1559, was a true ceremonial staircase used by the doge on his way to official ceremonies. Two doors open off the staircase which was reserved to illustrious personages and magistrates (one branch leads to the apartments of the doge). These doors lead to the **Sala degli Scudieri** (Pages' Room) and the **Sala del Magistrato al Criminal**.

The square drawing-room at the top of the Stairs contains works by J. Tintoretto (ceiling), Paolo Veronese and F. Bassano (on the walls). The left door leads to the **Cancelleria Ducale Superiore** and to the **Gran Cancelleria**, the one on the right to the **Room of the Four Doors** (delle Quattro Porte), a sort of antichamber for the **Anticollegio** and the **Collegio**.

The statue of Francesco I della Rovere.

The Scala d'Oro.

The Sala dell'Anticollegio.

The former was used by those who were to be received by the doge in the « collegio », the latter was where the encounters of the doge with the Signoria della Serenissima, the Salvi Grandi and those of « Terraferma ed agli ordini » (comprising the full College) took place. It was where affairs of State were discussed.

The corridor next to the *throne* leads to the **Antichiesetta** (Antichapel), a sort of passageway to the **Secret Archives** and the **Ufficio del Savio Cassiere**. In the **Chiesetta** or Chapel the doge participated in mass every day, entering through the door to the right of the altar which communicates with stairs going down to the apartment on the floor below.

The **Andito del Consiglio dei Dieci** and the following **Sala del Consiglio** (Hall of the Council of Ten) are also reached from the Room of the Four Doors. Next in line is the so-called **Hall of the Bussola** which takes its name from the screened-off wooden box in the right corner. It is to all extents the interior of the « Bocca di Leone » (Lion's Mouth) and was where the Fante dei Cai (the chief of Police) used to wait. The next room is that of the **Three Heads of the Consiglio dei Dieci**, chosen every month by the Council from its Ten members. The **Room of the State Inquisitors** is reached from here and then two corridors lead to the Prisons.

The corridor after the lefthand doorway of the Hall of the Bussola leads both to the **Hall of the Censors** and to the **Armeria** where what was salvaged from the destruction of 1797 has been collected in three halls (dedicated to Gattamelata, Morosini and Bragadin). The door at the back of the last hall leads to the doge's apartments consisting of various rooms. The doge's councilors waited in the **Sala degli Scarlatti** (named after the color of their robes). During his term of office, the arms of the prince were exhibited in the **Sala dello Scudo** or delle **Carte Geografiche**, and this is also where his bodyguards waited. The coat of arms now shown is that of the last doge, Ludovico Manin. The **Sala dei Filosofi** or Philosophers' Hall from which the doge had access to the stairs which led to the chapel owes its name to the twelve *Philosophers* painted by Veronese and Tintoretto, set in the walls before they were returned to the Libreria Vecchia (Sansovino Library). The **Sala degli Stucchi**, reached from the last door on the left, contains paintings by various masters, including Jacopo Tintoretto and G. B. Veneziano.

A door next to the fireplace (now walled up) led to the **Banquet Hall**. After the passage is the **Sala Erizzo**, a reception hall, followed by the **Sala Grimani** with a fine fireplace by the Lombardos.

Retracing one's steps and therefore recrossing the two rooms just described, we pass into the **Hall of the Quarantia Vecchia ai Civil** and the **Guariento Room** which was an arms deposit for the Maggior Consiglio. The remains of the *Paradise* painted by Guariento and damaged in the fire of 1577 are to be found here. The passage then leads to the **Sala del Maggior Consiglio**, or the Great Council Chamber, 54 m. long and 25 m. wide. All the nobles listed in the Libro d'oro who were over 25 years old automatically had the right to a seat, as well as thirty patricians between 25 and 30 years of age who were drawn by lot every year on the day of St. Barbara. An enormous canvas 7.65 m. by 24.6 m. dominates the back wall. Tintoretto painted it between 1588 and 1590 in the Scuola Vecchia della Misericordia. It has been restored more than once. Works by Veronese, Palma Giovane, A. Vicentini are also in the hall, on three sides of which runs a frieze with the *portraits of the doges*, two by two, painted by D. Tintoretto. Until 1902 many of the books of the Biblioteca Marciana were housed here.

The staircase that begins at the **Triumphal Arch** (honoring Doge Morosini, the Peloponnesiacus) leads down to the **Loggia Foscara** with a fine view of the Basilica, the Piazzetta, and

The Sala del Senato: a detail of the ceiling.

The interior of a cell in the prisons known as "i Pozzi".

The entrance corridor to the Prigioni Nuove.

the quay. This was where exhibitions were organized by the Congregations of Arts and Trades when the doge and dogaressa were crowned. The inner loggia (on the courtyard) then leads to the **Hall of the Censors**, a magistrature created in 1507 to keep an eye on possible election frauds. Access to the **Palazzo delle Prigioni** where the rooms have vaults in Istrian stone is from this room. A wooden staircase then leads to the « pozzi » or « wells » where the cells were marked with Roman numerals. The only cell that survived the destruction of 1797 is Roman numeral VII, still lined with wooden boards, a pallet in larch wood, and a small shelf.

The **Museo dell'Opera di Palazzo** on the ground floor has the original capitals from the exterior colonnade of the Doges Palace (replaced during restoration), some columns, reliefs and original fragments from the crenellation and the architrave of the Porta della Carta.

146

San Zaccaria, interior: the famous altarpiece by Bellini.

The Church of San Moisè.

CHURCH OF SAN ZACCARIA

The original Church of San Zaccaria dates to the 9th century but it was rebuilt after the fire of 1105 and transformed in Gothic style between the 15th and 16th centuries by Antonio Gambello and Mauro Codussi. The extremely tall **facade** has a large arched pediment as its crowning element with a row of blind niches and decorative panels. The lovely statue of *St. Zaccariah* over the portal is by Alessandro Vittoria.

The **interior** (with tall columns dividing the two side aisles from the nave in a perfect fusion of Gothic and Renaissance styles) contains an *altarpiece* by Giovanni Bellini, a *Madonna and Saints* by Palma Vecchio, the *Birth of the Baptist* by Tintoretto and the *Flight to Egypt* by G. D. Tiepolo. *Frescoes* by Andrea del Castagno are to be seen in the **San Tarasio Chapel**, as well as three *polyptychs* by Giovanni d'Alemagna and Antonio Vivarini. The sepulcher of A. Vittoria, with his *self-portrait*, is at the back of the left aisle. The two *holy water fonts* in the church as well as the statues of the *Baptist* and of *St. Zaccariah* near the entrance are by Vittoria. In his testa-

ment he also donated his house in Calle della Pietà to the nuns of San Zaccaria and asked to be buried in the church.

CHURCH OF SAN MOISÈ

The original 8th-century church was rebuilt in the 10th century for a certain Moisè Venier who wanted it dedicated to his patron saint. In the 14th century a **campanile** in brick with two-light openings in the belfry was added. The **facade**, which is particularly lovely, with a wealth of sculpture, is the work of Alessandro Tremignon and the sculptor Enrico Meyring and dates to the second half of the 17th century.

The church with its single nave contains many 17th- and 18th-century paintings. Carved wooden *choir stalls* dating to the 16th century are in the sanctuary. In the chapel on the left are a *Last Supper* by Palma Il Giovane and a *Washing of the Feet* by Jacopo Tintoretto.

The Church of Santa Maria Gloriosa dei Frari.

The Assumption by Titian.

CHURCH OF SANTA MARIA GLORIOSA DEI FRARI

Santa Maria Gloriosa dei Frari, a Franciscan church, was begun in 1250 apparently to plans by Nicola Pisano. It was enlarged and modified in 1338 by Scipione Bon. Romanesque-Gothic in style, the **facade** is divided into three parts by pilasters, with spires at the top. A statue by Alessandro Vittoria is set above the portal while the figures at the sides are by the School of Bon.

The **campanile** is next in height to that of San Marco and was built by the Celega in the 14th century. The **interior** of the church is Latin-cross in plan with twelve columns supporting tall arches set between the nave and the two side aisles. After the *Mausoleum of Titian*, note should be taken of the many fine works which enrich the church and make it perhaps the most famous place in Venice, after San Marco, and together with San Zanipolo the one containing the greatest number of the mortal remains of famous men. In the right aisle the *altar* by Longhena has two statues by Giusto Le Court; in the second bay is *Titian's tomb* (the artist died of the plague in 1576), made in 1852 by pupils of Antonio Canova. The third altar has sculpture by Alessandro Vittoria. To the right of the right transept is the *Monument to Admiral Jacopo Marcello*, by Pietro Lombardo. On the wall next to it is the *Monument to the Blessed Pacifico* with a fine bas-relief (the *Baptism of Christ*) by Bartolo and Michele da Firenze. In the **Sacristy** there is a stupendous triptych by Giovanni Bellini depicting the *Enthroned Madonna and Child with Music-making Angels and Saints* (1488). In the third chapel of the right apse is a *triptych* by Bartolomeo Vivarini.

The *Monument to Doge Francesco Foscari*, by the Bregno brothers (circa 1475), is in the chancel; on the left wall is the *Monument to Doge Nicolò Tron* by Antonio Rizzo. Behind the high altar rises the famous *Assumption* by Titian (1518). Of note in the first apse chapel to the left is a lovely *Madonna and Child* (1535) by Bernardo Licinio. In the third chapel is an altarpiece by Alvise Vivarini and Marco Basaiti with *St. Ambrose Enthroned*. In the fourth, particular attention goes to a *triptych* by Bartolomeo Vivarini and a *St. John Baptist* by Jacopo Sansovino on the baptismal font.

In the left aisle, on the second altar, is the *Madonna di Casa Pesaro*, an altarpiece by Titian (1526) with, further on, the *Monument to Doge Giovanni Pesaro*, by Longhena (1669) and the *Mausoleum to Antonio Canova*, planned by the master and executed by his pupils.

The Madonna of Ca' Pesaro by Titian.

CHURCH OF SAN GIORGIO MAGGIORE

San Giorgio Maggiore is one of Andrea Palladio's finest works (1565-1580). The **facade** is tripartite with columns and Corinthian capitals. The statues of *St. George* and *St. Stephen* are set into the two niches between the columns. In the wings are the *busts* by Giulio dal Moro. The **campanile** of 1791 is by Benedetto Buratti and was built to replace the one that fell in 1773.

The inverted Latin-cross interior has a nave and two aisles and a dome. Two splendid works by Tintoretto, a *Last Supper* and the *Gathering of the Manna*, are in the sanctuary. In the apse are fine wooden *choir stalls* of 1598 carved by the Flemish sculptor Van der Brulle.

The Church of San Giorgio Maggiore.

Francesco Guardi: The island of San Giorgio Maggiore.

GALLERIA DELL'ACCADEMIA

For a general view of the development of Venetian painting in the five centuries ranging from the 14th to the 18th century a visit to the Academy Gallery is essential. It was officially created as an « Accademia dei pittori e scultori » by a decree of the Republic of Venice on September 14, 1750. The first director was Giambattista Piazzetta and the headquarters were in the building which currently houses the Capitaneria di Porto. In 1807 it was decided to move it to the buildings of the Church of Santa Maria della Carità, the Scuola Grande of the same name, and the Monastero dei Canonici Lateranensi, forming the new « Accademia delle Belle Arti ». The old **Scuola della Confraternita** had been completed between the 14th and the 15th centuries. The facade was now renovated by Maccarozzi in neoclassic style on a project by Giorgio Massari. The **Church of Santa Maria della Carità** was on the site of a precedent Romanesque structure; the workshop of Bartolomeo Bon was involved in the new structure which dates to between 1441 and 1452. The third building, the **Convent of the Lateran Canons**, is one of the finest examples of Palladian architecture in Venice. These buildings were adapted to their new function by Antonio Selva who had what was left of the Corinthian atrium and the short sides of the cloister torn down, replacing them with a double loggia so as to connect the rooms of the convent with those of the church.

The original core of the present collection dates to the 18th century and was comprised of the paintings submitted by the aspiring academicians. From the time of its refounding one donation followed the other, both by private individuals — in particular the Contarini bequest of 1838 and the Renier legacy of 1850 — and the « forced » donations of the religious institutions repressed by Napoleon, as well as additions, in more recent times, due to acquisitions on the part of the State. An important group of paintings, chosen by Peter Edwards, president of the old Accademia from 1793-1796, was bought in 1812. Works by Carpaccio, the Bellinis, Titian, Pordenone, and Paolo Veronese were acquired in the years immediately after. When Napoleon fell, the Louvre had to return works by Paris Bordone, Jacopo Tintoretto, and the *Supper in the House of Levi* which Paolo Veronese had painted in 1537 for the Refectory of the Convent of Santi Giovanni e Paolo.

As already stated, the rooms provide a complete panorama of Venetian painting, beginning with works still of Byzantine inspiration. This period, up to the 14th century, is well represented by examples which include polyptychs by the Veneziano's — Catarino's *Coronation of the Virgin* dating to 1375, and the *Annunciation, Saints and Prophets* by Lorenzo of 1357. There are also works by Iacobello del Fiore, Jacobello Alberegno and Nicolò di Pietro.

The 15th century is also represented by outstanding paintings, including Giovanni Bellini's *Madonna and Child between St. Catherine and the Magdalen, Enthroned Madonna Adoring the Sleeping Child in her Lap*, and the entire cycle of the *Legend of St. Orsola* by Carpaccio, originally painted

Giorgione (Giorgio da Castelfranco): The Tempest.

for the oratory of the Scuola di Sant'Orsola. There are also numerous works by Vivarini, G. D'Alemagna, Lazzaro Bastiani.

For the 16th century of particular note is Giorgione's most famous painting, *The Tempest*, as well as what remains of his fresco showing a *Nude* that originally decorated the facade of the Fondaco dei Tedeschi. Then there is Titian's *Pietà* and his *Presentation of the Virgin in the Temple*, Paolo Veronese's *Supper in the House of Levi* and his *Madonna and Child with Saints*, as well as the stupendous *Miracle of St. Mark* and *Adam and Eve* by Jacopo Tintoretto. There is also a rich assortment of works by minor artists, Boccaccino, Lorenzo Lot-

to, Paris Bordone, Schiavone, Pordenone.

Works by Bernardo Strozzi, *Banquet in the House of the Pharisee* and *Saint Jerome*; the *Parable of the Good Samaritan* by Domenico Fetti; Mazzoni's *Annunciation*, as well as paintings by Maffei and others cover the 17th century.

The 18th century is particularly well represented, with some of the most important works of Venetian artists, including Pietro Longhi's *Philosopher*, the *Fortune-teller* and a *Crucifixion* by G. B. Piazzetta, *Portrait of a Young Man* and a *Self-Portrait* by Rosalba Carriera, *St. Joseph with the Child and other Saints* by G. B. Tiepolo, and finally Canaletto's *Porticato*.

155

MUSEO DEL SETTECENTO VENEZIANO

The Museum of the Venetian Eighteenth Century is in **Palazzo Rezzonico** in the sestriere of Dorsoduro.
In 1935 the palace was bought by the City of Venice which restored and refurbished the interior as a splendid aristocratic Venetian 18th-century home.

The **Ballroom** — entrance to which is via a *staircase* by G. Massari — with stupendous carved furniture by Brustolon, leads to the **Room of the Allegory of Marriage**, named after the fresco by Tiepolo depicting the *Wedding of Ludovico Rezzonico*, from the **Room of the Pastels** with works by Rosalba Carriera, to the **Hall of Tapestries**, with 17th-century Flemish *tapestries*; from the **Throne Room**, formerly nuptial chamber with a fresco by Tiepolo, to the Hall dedicated to him where he painted the large fresco with *Fortune* and *Wisdom*: from the **Library Hall** with *canvases of mythological subjects* by Maffei to the **Sala del Lazzarini** and that **of Brustolon** with beautiful pieces of inlaid furniture made by the master from Belluno who was particularly active in Venice. On the second floor the **Portego dei Dipinti**, with works by Piazzetta, Jan Liss and Giuseppe Zais, leads to the **Sala del Longhi** with 34 pictures of *life in Venice*. The *ceiling* is by Tiepolo. After two smaller rooms, frescoed by Guardi, comes the perfect reconstruction of an 18th-century bedroom. Two more small rooms, and the visitor finds himself in a reconstruction of the villa at Zianigo with frescoes by Gian Domenico Tiepolo.

Of particular interest on the second floor are the **Room of the Clowns**, the **Chapel** frescoed by Tiepolo in 1749, and the **Sala del Ridotto** (Gaming room) with the famous small paintings by Guardi, the *Parlatorio delle Monache* (Nuns' Parlor) and the *Sala del Ridotto*.

The small **Room of the Stuccoes** is particularly charming. Just as interesting on the third floor is the reconstruction of an old pharmacy or Chemist's Shop and a Marionette Theater, with a collection of 18th-century Venetian marionettes.

Anonymous 17th-century painter: Allegory of the Holy Alliance (Museo Correr).

GALLERIA FRANCHETTI

The collection is situated on the upper floors of the **Ca' d'Oro**, and to get there one must first cross a fine courtyard — entrance to which is from the Grand Canal, through a lovely Gothic *four-light opening* — embellished by a 15th-century marble *well-head* before climbing an open staircase resting on Gothic arches. The ground floor portico is surrounded by various Roman and Hellenistic *statues* and has a mosaic pavement. The **Quadreria** (Picture Gallery) displays works by Antonio Vivarini, Vittore Carpaccio, Paris Bordone, Alessandro Vittoria, Titian, Mantegna — his splendid painting of *St. Sebastian* —, Van Dyck, Pontormo, Filippo Lippi, Francesco Guardi, Luca Signorelli, Van Eyck, Tintoretto, Sansovino. The Gallery now also contains the frescoes by Campagnola and Pordenone which were removed from the walls of the cloister of Santo Stefano, as well as old Venetian ceramics from the 11th to the 18th centuries including the famous fragments of the Conton collection.

Other rooms annexed to the Gallery belong to the Palazzo Giusti, which is next to the Ca' d'Oro. These three rooms contain bronzes of Venetian school and other examples of Flemish and Dutch art. Note should be taken in passing from the first to the second floor of the Ca' d'Oro of a splendid carved wooden *staircase*, originally in the Agnello House.

MUSEO CIVICO CORRER

The Museo Civico Correr is situated in the **Napoleonic Wing of the Procuratie Nuove**. Formed around an original nucleus of paintings given in 1830 by the Venetian patrician Teodoro Correr. The entire conspicuous patrimony of the Correr collection has been divided into three sections, two of which are installed elsewhere: the Museum of the Venetian Eighteenth Century (Settecento) in Ca' Rezzonico and the Archaeological Museum in another wing of the Procuratie Nuove with an entrance from the Piazzetta. The Museo Correr is dedicated to the Historical Collections, the Picture Gallery and the Museum of the Risorgimento.

Francesco Guardi: Grand Canal with church of the Salute (Galleria Franchetti).

Francesco Guardi: Piazzetta S. Marco (Galleria Franchetti).

MURANO

This typical settlement in the lagoon spreads out over five islands and was created by refugees from Opiterga and Altino fleeing from the Huns and Lombards. It developed rapidly and as early as 1275 was already governed by a Venetian podestà but with regulations of its own. For centuries it was considered the vacation site for the patrician families of Venice, and as a result churches and palaces were built and rebuilt.

Glass making, for which Murano has become famous throughout the world, has ancient beginnings. In 1292 all the glass factories of Venice were transferred to Murano so as to protect the city from the danger of fire. With the affirmation of blown glass and the development of other techniques such as milk glass, Murano reached its zenith in the 15th century.

Glassblowing in Murano.

The apse of the Church of SS. Maria e Donato.

A typical corner of Burano.

The famous lace of Burano.

BURANO

The original settlement of Burano was on a different island, closer to the sea, and it was probably due to some natural calamity that the community of Burano later moved to « *Vicus Buranis* », on the island near Mazzorbo. Life on the island, which counted about 8,000 souls, was bound to Torcello up to the 18th century, when Torcello went into its fatal decline. Life on Burano was always characterized by its relation with art. The musician B. Galuppi was born here in 1706 and it was a fertile point of encounter for painters above all in the 20th century.

The most important economic activity of Burano is a felicitous encounter of art and craft: the lace which reached its zenith between the 16th and 17th centuries, thanks also to the protection granted by the Dogaresses Giovanna Duodo and Morosina Morosini. There was a decline in lace-making in the 18th century until a school was established in the 1880s and 90s.

There are two churches on the island: the church of **San Martino** founded in the 16th century and the church of **Santa Maria delle Grazie**, set on the site of a chapel of Doge Grimani. It was closed as a church in 1810 and is now used as a social center.

NAPLES

The mere mention of the words "Gulf of Naples" immediately conjours up a kaleidoscope of brilliant pictures; varied, vivid, well-defined and often contrasting, but all having in common a wide and profoundly intense involvement of the senses, usually mixed with high-flown sentiments. The natural surroundings of this area, which for thousands of years have borne the indelible stamp of the presence of man, reveal primordial aspects which arouse feelings of amazement and marvel interspersed with anxiety and solicitude. If on the one hand the unparalleled stimulation gained from the Mediterranean environment has always aroused wonder in tourists from all over the world, on the other hand the vulcanic nature of the Parthenopean gulf, the instability of the terrafirma in the large southern metropolis, the disturbing questions raised by the Flegrean region - not to mention "himself", the sombre lord of the gulf who, under the guise of a serene and peaceful mountain rules over the fortunes of a much wider territory which is heavily populated - cannot do other than induce us to reflect on how many people are involved in safeguarding and preserving one of the more beautiful corners of this wonderful country.

The classical authors of the Latinity called it "Campania Felix"; "lucky" Campania, from time immemorial, because of the extraordinary fertility of its vulcanic soil, the unrivaled mildness of its gentle Mediterranean climate and the unique splendour of its extremely rich and varied countryside. In this ancient and singular region Naples and its gulf play a primary role. Less than 39 kms separate Mount Cuma, on the most westerly point of the Flegrean Fields, from Punta Campanella, situated on the end of the Sorrento peninsula. Along this perfect arc are to be found the pearls of the picturesque and evocative Parthenopean "necklace": the Flegrean Islands - Ischia, Procida and Vivara- Bacoli, Miseno, Baia, Cuma, Pozzuoli and the Solfatara crater, Naples and Vesuvius, Castellammare di Stabia, Sorrento and its coast and Capri.

This fan-shaped area, which is itself a ricin and exhaustive source of propositions, acts as a starting point for other tourist itineraries and destinations, which each visitor can adapt to his own needs and specific interests. The Gulf of Naples district contains an exceptional amount of art and historical works, besides a superlative open-air nature museum. Evidence of man's evolution - from the beginning of the Roman era, through the Dark Ages, up to the troubled present times, ending with the contradictions and unsolved problems of contemporary society - is forceably placed in the natural surroundings which act as a backdrop to the remains of the past and to the bold and futuristic architectural solutions which have been brought to completion during the past few decades.

Those who wish to understand the real nature of Naples and its numerous tourist sites must necessarily look beyond certain obsolete and outworn stereotypes such as the sun, the pizza, the spaghetti and the tarantella. Even if the Parthenopean gulf region is without a shadow of doubt among the sunnier spots in the Mediterranean, even if its sea and its sky are among the bluer and more serene in Italy, even if the splendour of its coast and the lush vegetation gratify the senses of the visitor, it is however necessary to investigate its cultural aspects. These go deeper than its treasures in art, history, architecture and craftsmanship, even though these take a major role, and descend into the realms of folklore and popular traditions; into that genuine and outspoken culture which invented the pizza and the Neapolitan song but which has always had its own indomitable identity, in spite of the various dominating powers. The art of making-do and picking up the pieces to start out afresh, the ancestral desire to infringe the rules and mix the sacred with the profane-like the blood of San Gennaro (St. Januarius) and the lottery numbers, the pyrotechnical and liberating joie de vivre, Piedigrotta or the events of the local football team - have become part of a custom which cannot be denied.

arch is a complex structure made up of an archway flanked by Corinthian columns placed side by side (in the intrados there is some relief work depicting *Alfonso among Relations and Dignitaries of the Kingdom*); these columns support an attic storey which holds the splendid sculptural representations of *Alfonso I making his Triumphal Entrance into Naples*. Above the attic is a second arch which opens between coupled Ionic columns; these support a second attic decorated with niches containing the statues of *Temperance*, *Strength*, *Justice* and *Magnamity*. Dominating this remarkable achievement is a semi-circular tympanum bearing the allegorical representation of two rivers, and above this stands the statue of the *Archangel Michael*. The most prominent names of those responsible for the admirable cycle of sculptures include Francesco Laurana, Domenico Gagini, Isaia da Pisa, and Pére Johan. Having been renovated and modified several times (16th-18th centuries), the Maschio Angioino today displays the 15th-century appearance it assumed following conservative restoration work carried out in the first half of the 20th century.

The **Palatine Chapel**, with its square plan, is characterised by its cross vaulting, with windows very similar to those of the church of Santa Chiara. The chapel is also known as the *Church of Santa Barbara* or *San Sebastiano* and is said to have been painted by Giotto, but very little remains of this work. Inside the chapel some interesting sculptures by Laurana and Andrea dell'Aquila can be seen, as well as traces of frescoes by Maso di Banco. The **Museo Civico di Castelnuovo,** is situated in the **St Barbara Hall** and on the two floors above this in the eastern wing of the castle of the same name, better known as Maschio Angioino. The museum contains a collection of 14th-century frescoes, as well as paintings, sculptures and valuable silver work. Most of the 14th-century frescoes come from the Castello di Casaluce, in the province of Caserta. Others from the 15th century were brought here from the Neapolitan Church of the Annunziata which has been in disuse for many years. The St Barbara Hall contains fragments of sculptures by Neapolitan artists, produced around the middle of the 15th century, as well as tabernacles by Jacopo della Pila and Domenico Gagini, and statues by other artists from the same period (of special note is the *Virgin Mary with Child* by Laurana). Of particular interest on the second floor is the panel painting by an unknown Neapolitan from the 15th century. There are also works by important artists such as Battistello Caracciolo, Mattia Preti, Francesco Solimena and Francesco Jerace. The silver exhibits are also on this floor: of particular note among the most valuable and beautiful ones is the *Blessed Virgin* by Giuliano Finelli, a 17th-century artist from Carrara, and a St Barbara by Lelio Ciliberto. The third floor contains two magnificent works by Vincenzo Gemito, the *Boy's Head*, and the *Fisherman*.

Maschio Angioino: details of the Triumphal Arch.

The impressive façade of the Royal Palace.

PALAZZO REALE
(Royal Palace)

This harmonious structure dominates *Piazza del Plebiscito.* It was built to a design by the architect Domenico Fontana and work was begun on the construction in 1600 to coincide with the arrival in Naples of King Philip II. The building work lasted for more than fifty years; during the final phase the imposing staircase at the main entrance was completed. The palace was renovated and extended in the

first half of the 18th century, and restored by Gaetano Genovese who brought about some substantial neo-classical transformations to the building, following a fire which had damaged it at the time of Ferdinand II (1837). The last restoration work was carried out in 1994 when the palace hosted the 'summit' of the G7 (the seven most industrialised countries in the world). The impressive **façade,** above which stands a clock with a small ribbed campanile, contains two mighty rows of windows, alternating with pilaster strips. On the ground floor, the original portico was partly modified by Vanvitelli for reasons to do with the building's stability. There are three entrances on the ground floor. On the outside, the niches built by Vanvitelli contain statues of Naples' most important sovereign. In the entrance-hall, near the beautiful 17th-century grand staircase by Picchiatti, modified by Genovese, is a bronze door transferred here from the Maschio Angioino. Some of the palace wings now house various offices, while the **National Library** has been housed here since 1804, containing thousands of volumes and an important collection of papyri from Herculaneum. Other halls of importance include the **Central Hall,** the **Throne Room**, and the **Hercules Hall**, all of which, along with many other rooms of the Royal Apartment, make up an authentic museum (**The Royal Palace Historic Apartment Museum**). Note especially the works by Titian, Guercino, Andrea Vaccaro, Mattia Preti, Spagnoletto, Massimo Stanzione, and Luca Giordano.

A sumptuous hall in the Royal Palace.

BASILICA OF SAN FRANCESCO DI PAOLA

Constructed in imitation of the Pantheon in Rome, this church was built as an *ex voto* by Ferdinand I for having regained his lost reign. According to records, the first stone was laid in 1817 but the building was not completed until 29 years later. It was designed by the architect Pietro Bianchi. The church is raised above street level and looks onto *Piazza del Plebiscito,* opposite the Royal Palace. Its dome is 53 metres high and is flanked by two smaller side domes. The pronaos on the **façade** culminates in a triangular tympanum on which stand the statues representing *Religion, St Ferdinand of Castiglia* and *St Francis of Paola.* The imposing colonnade, which gives the square its attractive semi-circular appearance, was designed by Leopoldo Laperuta (early 19th century). The interior, with its circular plan, contains a fine high altar decorated with an abundance of semi-precious stones, and numerous sculptures and paintings. The high altar was designed by Fuga, the architect who planned the majestic building in Piazza Carlo III, used for many years as an almshouse.

Piazza del Plebiscito and a night view of the Basilica of San Francesco di Paola.

The Galleria Umberto I.

The façade of the Church of San Ferdinando.

GALLERIA UMBERTO I

Situated between the San Carlo Theatre and *Via Toledo*, the arcade was built to eliminate a series of ill-famed alley-ways. It now bears the neo-Renaissance features given to it by Antonio Curri and Ernesto Di Mauro who, between 1887 and 1890, completed the design drawn up by the engineer Emanuele Rocco. The **interior** is distinguished by its central octagonal plan and assymmetrical cross-shape, embellished by its polychrome marble floor. In the centre, a large decoration shows the *Signs of the Zodiac* and a *Compass with the Cardinal Points*. The barrel-vaulted ceiling is made of long panes of glass, while a large dome opens in the centre.

CHURCH OF SAN FERDINANDO

Built in the 17th century to a design by Giovanni Conforto, the church was entrusted to the Company of Jesus. When the Jesuits were expelled from Naples, the building was donated to the Order of Constantine and dedicated to the saint whose namesake was the King of Naples, Ferdinand IV. Now famous as being the place of worship preferred by Neapolitan artists and writers who meet in the nearby arcade, the church contains some important works of art: in particular, the marble statues of *David and Moses* by Lorenzo and Domenico Antonio Vaccaro. Most of the frescoes were painted by Paolo De Matteis. Note also the *Tomb of Lucia Migliaccio*, Duchess of Floridia and the morganatic wife of Ferdinand I, by Tito Angelini.

SAN CARLO THEATRE

Its construction was commissioned by King Charles III of Bourbon who entrusted the direction of the work to Giovanni Antonio Medrano. The theatre was inaugurated on 4th November 1737, the King's Saint's day. At the request of the King, the man in charge of the work, Angelo Carasale, linked the theatre to the Royal Palace so that the King could directly back to the palace when performances were over. In 1816 the theatre was almost completely destroyed by fire, and King Ferdinand IV commissioned Antonio Niccolini with its reconstruction. Its greatest merit, however, is its near-perfect acoustics, making the San Carlo one of the most coveted theatres for leading opera singers and conductors.

The interior of the San Carlo Theatre; on the ceiling, Apollo introducing the poets to Minerva, *by Giuseppe Cammarano.*

FONTANA DEL NETTUNO
(Neptune's Fountain)

One of the finest examples of Neapolitan urban decoration, this fountain, which was situated opposite the dockyard, has stood in *Piazza Bovio* (or *Piazza Borsa*) since 1898. It was built to a design by Giovanni Domenico D'Auria at the beginning of the 17th century by Domenico Fontana. Fanzago added the balustrade with its *lions* and coats of arms. Most of the sculptures (*Nymphs, Sea-horses, Satires* and *Tritons*) are the work of Pietro Bernini, while *Neptune with Trident* is attributed to Michelangelo Naccherino.

FONTANA DELL'IMMACOLATELLA
(Fountain of the Blessed Virgin)

Standing between *Via Nazario Sauro* and *Via Partenope* on the waterfront, this fountain dates from 1601 and was created by M. Naccherino and P. Bernini. It was situated in *Piazza del Plebiscito*. The fountain takes its name from the nearby **Stazione Marittima dell'Immacolatella.** One of the most widely reproduced images of Naples, it represents one of the symbols of the seafront of Naples, together with the Maschio Angioino and the Castel dell'Ovo.

FONTANA DEL SEBETO
(Fountain of the Sebeto)

Continuing along the waterfront we come to *Largo Sermoneta* where the 17th-century Fontana del Sebeto stands. It was built by Carlo Fanzago and was originally situated on the *Salita del Gigante* which led to *Piazza del Plebiscito*. In 1939 it was transferred to its present position. The fountain consists of a central basin with dolphins and an *Allegory of the River Sebeto* which once flowed through the city.

Right, from top to bottom, the fountains of the Immacolatella and of the Sebeto; below, the nice Neptune's Fountain in Piazza Giovanni Bovio.

CASTEL DELL'OVO

Built on the small island of Magaride, Castel dell'Ovo rises up in the centre of the gulf, between the marina of Mergellina and the Borgo Marinaro, a short distance from the Villa Comunale. In Roman times the site was occupied by the *Castrum Lucullium,* a fort belonging to the Roman patrician, Lucius Licinus Lucullus. During the centuries which followed, the Normans and the Angevins extended and fortified the tuff building. The castle was the royal residence of Charles I of Anjou and of Alfonso of Aragon, and in the 17th century it was converted into a prison. The monk and philosopher Tommaso Campanella was among those imprisoned here. The castle is well worth visiting. Note especially the bastions constructed in yellow tuff, the **Monks' Refectory**, and the splendid view of the gulf from the terraces on the upper levels, taking in the promontory of Posillipo and the island of Capri which rises up in front of it. According to a medieval legend, the Roman poet Virgil, who in ancient times was considered a powerful wizard, hid an egg inside a jug hanging in one of the rooms of the castle. Tradition has it that when the jug containing the egg falls and breaks, the castle and the entire city will fall to ruin. The **interior** of the fortress contains medieval structures and includes examples of both Gothic style and much older remains, such as the ruins of a place of worship named after *San Salvatore*. Also worthy of note are the **Torre Maestra** ('Master Tower') and the **Torre Normandia** ('Normandy Tower').

Castel dell'Ovo from the Porto di Santa Lucia and another view of the imposing castle.

Monastery of Santa Chiara: two details of the cloister of the Poor Clares, tiled with majolica.

CHURCH OF SANTA CHIARA

The church of Santa Chiara stands against the Roman walls. It was built by Queen Sancia of Majorca, wife of Robert of Anjou. Sancia decided to have the convent and the adjoining church built because she could not enter the enclosed nuns' order herself. She entrusted the work to Gagliardo Primario (1310). Built in Gothic style, the Church of Santa Chiara has undergone numerous transformations. The church and adjoining **Convent** are run by the Friars Minor, while the enclosed Poor Clares occupy the **Monastery of the Holy Trinity** which borders on Santa Chiara, and the small church which looks onto *Piazza del Gesù*. The church façade bears a rose window of more than 8 metres in diameter. The **interior** preserves the *Tomb of Robert I of Anjou*. The work forms part of the Royal Tombs, which include the *Tomb of Mary of Durazzo*, the *Tombs of Mary of Valois and Charles of Calabria*, the *Tombs of Clemenza and Agnes of Durazzo*, and the *Penna Tomb*. The seventh chapel on the right contains the 14th-century *Balzo Tombs* and a *St Francis* by Naccherino. Several Bourbon sovereigns are buried in the tenth chapel. Note the *Tomb of Philip of Bourbon*, and that of *Maria Christina of Savoy*, wife of Ferdinand II. The high altar is dominated by a wooden *Crucifix* (14th century). Near the entrance is the *Tomb of Salvo D'Acquisto*, the sergeant of the Carabinieri who, with the sacrifice of his own life (23-9-1943) saved the lives of 22 people held hostage by the Germans. Behind the church is the **Poor Clares' Chancel,** an outstanding testimony of Gothic architecture. Note the fragments of frescoes painted by Giotto and students. Not far from the church stands the **Campanile**, built in the 14th century. Visitors to Santa Chiara should certainly not miss the old Majolica-tiled **Cloister** with designs of *Flowers and fruit* and *Scenes of Daily Life* .

The Church of the Gesù Nuovo, built on the site of the Palazzo dei Sanseverino; below: the Baroque Guglia dell'Immacolata.

PIAZZA DEL GESÙ NUOVO

The square is reached via *Calata Trinità Maggiore* and is found in the historic city centre, representing a meeting point between the Medieval and Renaissance eras, and Baroque Naples. Situated in the square are **Palazzo Pignatelli, Palazzo Sanfelice,** and the **Church of the Gesù Nuovo**. On one side stands the majestic Gothic complex of the **Monastery** and **Church of Santa Chiara**. The **Guglia dell'Immacolata** (*'Column of the Blessed Virgin'*) dates from 1750. It was designed by Giuseppe Genuino and the work was directed by Giuseppe Di Fiore. The sculptural decoration on the column by Matteo Bottiglieri and Francesco Pagani is an example of Neapolitan Baroque. At the top stands a statue in gilded copper of the *Immacolata (Blessed Virgin)*, dating from 1753. Every year on 8th December, the feast of the 'Immacolata', firemen place a wreath of flowers at the statue's feet, at the top of the column.

CHURCH OF THE GESÙ NUOVO

Strongly characterised by the Baroque style, the Church of the Gesù Nuovo was built by Giuseppe Valeriano on the site of the Palazzo dei Sanseverino (16th-17th century). The church follows a Greek cross plan and consists of nave and aisles of unequal length. The typical diamond-pointed rusticated **façade,** by Novello da San Lucano, belonged to the Sanseverino Palace. The **interior** is marked by the great use made of marble polychromy, and the floor, also made of marble, merits equal attention. There are some notable works of art by Cosimo Fanzago, Luca Giordano and Francesco Solimena. The **Chapel of St Anne** is particularly interesting with its 64 wooden reliquary busts of saints.

CATHEDRAL

A visit to Naples is unthinkable without a stop at at least the most important churches, for they are precious keepers of invaluable works of art and testify to the city's glorious history. A tour of these churches should begin at the Cathedral, the centre of the city's religious life. Inside is the Chapel of St Januarius containing the relics of this saint, the patron of Campania. Named after *Our Lady of the Assumption,* the cathedral was built on the site of the earlier Stefania, a 6th-century basilica whose remains can still be seen in the adjoining Palazzo Vescovile (Archbishop's Palace). Situated on the same site were the Basilica of Santa Restituta, the twin building of the Stefania (4th century), and the seat of Asprenus, the first Bishop of Naples, who was subsequently elevated to sainthood. The construction of the Cathedral was actually ordered by Charles I of Anjou, although many historians maintain that it was his son, Charles II, who requested its building.

The **façade** was destroyed by the 1349 earthquake and was completely rebuilt over the centuries. The neo-Gothic style now predominates, as intended by the designer Enrico Alvino. However, the most recent reconstruction work was carried out in 1951 and 1969 in order to repair the serious damage caused by the bombings of 1943. The portals of the church are in 15th-century style and are the work of the sculptor Antonio Baboccio (1407). Note the main portal, decorated with Lions supporting columns (14th century), and a *Madonna* by Tino di Camaino. The interior follows a Latin cross plan with aisles, sustained by 16 piers supporting a total of 110 antique granitic columns. The *Monument to Charles I, Charles Martel* and *Clementina of Habsburg,* which stands out in the double façade, was created at the end of the 16th century by Domenico Fontana. The *Christening Font* is a fine work of the 17th century. Of particular note in the right-hand transept is the altar-piece of *Our Lady of the Assumption,* by Perugino. To the right of the presbytery (second chapel), lies the Minutolo Chapel, a fine example of Gothic architecture. It is distinguished by the Minutolo Tombs and a series of beautiful frescoes and paintings, said to be the work of Montano d'Arezzo and Roberto d'Oderisio.

The neo-Gothic façade of the Cathedral of San Gennaro.

The precious reliquary-bust of San Gennaro and an aspect of the liquefaction of the blood of the Saint.

The Baptismal Font.

To the left of the presbytery (second chapel), is the **Chapel of St Lawrence,** with its Jesse Tree, a valuable fresco by Lello da Orvieto (14th century). The polygonal apse dates from the 18th century, while the four transept chapels preserve their original Gothic appearance. Of particular interest are the four paintings in the transept, and the 14th-century bishop's throne in marble (situated beneath the left-hand organ). The Cathedral also contains many tombs of illustrious figures including *St Asprenus.* Below the high altar is the Cathedral's **Succorpo,** a small chapel, also known as the *Confession of St Januarius* or the *Carafa Chapel.* It is maintained that Bramante contributed to its design. It is reached via a double staircase which is closed by two bronze doors and was commissioned in 1497 by Cardinal Oliviero Carafa. The relics of St Januarius are kept here. They are contained in an urn at the altar, opposite which is the Statue of Cardinal Oliviero Carafa at Prayer by the local artist G. T. Malvito.

The construction of the **Chapel of the Treasury of St Januarius** (San Gennaro) was begun on 7th June 1608 to a design by Francesco Grimaldi, to fulfil a vow made by the city which some decades earlier had been threatened by the plague. The brass entrance gate was designed by Cosimo Fanzago in 1630. The chapel follows a Greek cross plan and is surmounted by a dome. Its sumptuous decoration consists of precious marble, silver and paintings. The dome was painted in the 17th century by Lanfranco *(Heaven);* the remaining frescoes are the work of Domenichino *(Episodes from the Life of St Januarius).* The paintings on copper at the altar are by Domenichino and Ribera. The high altar was built to a design by Solimena and is completely covered with silver and gilded copper decorations. In front of this are two beautifully made silver candelabras. Behind the high altar there is a safe with two keys, one in the possession of the Cardinal of Naples and the other with the Mayor (who is the head of the Treasury delegation) - the safe contains the two phials of the martyr's blood which are displayed to the public twice a year - in September and on the Sunday before the first Sunday of May - when the liquefaction miracle repeats itself. It is on this occasion that the exquisite *Reliquary Bust* is displayed to the public; it was made in the city in the 14th century by the French Masters Etienne, Godefroyd, Guillaume de Verdelay, and Milet d'Auxerre. It is considered to be one of the masterpieces of Gothic goldsmith's art from beyond the Alps.

The **Sacristy,** entirely painted by Giordano and Farelli, contains the *Bust of St Januarius* cloaked in a red cope, and 44 silver busts of the co-patron saints of Naples. Up until a few years ago these statues were paraded through the streets of the old town centre - from the Cathedral to Santa Chiara - to celebrate the "May Miracle" which commemorates the removal of the saint's remains from Montevergine, in the province of Avellino, to Naples.

The **Church of Santa Restituta** was built around 334. It is situated within the Cathedral and is reached via the entrance opposite the Treasury Chapel. Not much remains of the original structure, the ancient Constantine Basilica with its Latin cross plan. Some Baroque details were added to the building's characteristic Byzantine style during the most recent restoration work around the end of the 17th century. The entire building rests on 17 Corinth columns. The chapel contains the body of St Restituta, of African origins, who together with St John is the patron of the island of Ischia. Note the mosaic of the *Madonna with Child Enthroned between Saints Januarius and Restituta* by Lello da Orvieto.

Of particular artistic interest is the **Chapel of San Giovanni** which used to be the baptistery. Otherwise known as **San Giovanni in Fonte,** it dates from the 4th-5th centuries. The building is square in form and opens at one end into the Church of Santa Restituta. Note in particular the splendid mosaic decorations, created at the time of the baptistry's foundation.

Detail of the Chapel of San Gennaro.

The imposing interior of the Cathedral.

The exterior of the Museo Archeologico Nazionale.

The marble Statue of a Nereid, one of the masterpieces on exhibit in the Archaeological Museum.

MUSEO ARCHEOLOGICO NAZIONALE
(National Archaeological Museum)

The National Archaeological Museum can be considered one of the most important cultural centres in the world in terms of the quantity and quality of Greek and Roman relics it contains. The museum building was constructed in 1585, on the hill of Santa Teresa. Originally a Cavalry Barracks, it was later used as a University, and was finally turned into a museum. The National Library was situated here for a long period, up until 1922 when it was transferred to the Royal Palace. The initial nucleus of the museum was established by Charles of Bourbon to display the Farnese collections which he inherited from his mother. However, the subsequent enlargement of the immense artistic patrimony determined by the addition of remains found in the archaeological excavations at Pompeii, Herculaneum and Stabia, led to the search for new premises, and the tranfer to the present building. It is practically impossible to mention every one of the enormous number of relics and works on display here. Most notable among the various exhibits and rooms are the *Farnese Hercules*, from the Roman Baths of Caracalla and the *Farnese Cup*, a splendid example of cameo, once a part of the Medici collections. Completing the vast array of exhibits are paintings from Pompeii, Herculaneum and Stabia, sculptures, small bronzes, and a collection of vases. Among the latter, note the vases originating from Etruria, Attica, Lucania, Apulia and Campania.

Pozzuoli: the so-called Temple of Serapis, actually a public market of the Roman period.

Below, the Flavian Amphitheatre. Its construction was carried out by the emperor Vespasian in the second half of the 1st century A.D. As to dimensions, it is the third in Italy after the Colosseum in Rome and the amphitheatre at Santa Maria Capua Vetere.

POZZUOLI

Pozzuoli is one of the oldest centres in Campania. It was founded in 520 BC as *Dikaearchia* and was originally a port for Cumae and later for the Romans who changed its name to *Puteoli*.

The town is full of ancient relics, including the remains of the **Roman Port,** the **Temple of Augustus,** the **Temple of Serapis** and the **Amphitheatre,** as well as other marvels such as the **Church of St Januarious** (San Gennaro) where the patron of Naples was decapitated in 305. It is here that, twice a year, a miracle takes place, consisting in the liquefaction of dried blood on a stone in the church.

Also in Pozzuoli is the **Solfatara,** the crater of a volcano which allows visitors to enter a lunar landscape where jets of carbon dioxide and hot mud give the area a rather fascinating appearance.

Then there is the **Rione Terra**, a completely deserted area of the town, perched on a spur above the port and consisting of an inextricable maze of narrow streets. It was abandoned following the onset of the phenomenon of negative bradyseism (the gradual rising of the land) which had compromised the stability of the buildings.

The archaeological site of Pompeii.

Below, a millstone, architectural fragments, stone weights and amphorae inside the Horrea or Forum Olitorium (Warehouses and grain markets).

Above, a section of the via Stabiana; below, the interior of the ►
Basilica with the "Tribunal" in the background.

POMPEII

The story of humanity is full of moving and touching episodes: the rediscovery, or more precisely the resurrection, of Pompeii and Herculaneum are among the most important. Today Mt. Vesuvius, in all its calm majesty, looms over the countryside speckled with spots of greenery and houses: grapevines cling to its ample sides and the broom once more flowers. It is hard to imagine today that this serenely beautiful landscape was once the setting for tragedy and death, violence and destruction.

But the ruins of Pompeii and Herculaneum stand as witnesses. For what happened in Pompeii and Herculaneum may be unique in history: not only did a civilization die here, as was the case elsewhere in analogous situations, but daily life came to a sudden standstill. People died on the thresholds of their houses, the loaves of bread stayed in the oven, and the dogs remained chained outside the door and the slaves in their bonds. The coins still lay on the table in the taverne, and the papyrus scrolls on the shelves of the libraries. These walls still bear the election slogans and phrases of love and of derision.

The catastrophe took place so unexpectedly that the daily course of life, the activities of hundreds and hundreds of people, was suddenly interrupted. Nor does it mean much that death came differently to Herculaneum and to Pompeii. Little does it matter if here there was a hope, the barest hope, of

Above, fresco with cupids in the House of the Vettii; right, the bronze statue in the Temple of Apollo.

Above, the atrium in the House of the Faun; below, the ruins of the Forum portico.

flight, while rivers of mud flowed down and covered the city, while there the chances of escaping from the sulphurous vapors and the impalpable layer of ashes which slowly suffocated and covered everything were null. Their fate was the same, they were condemned, the two of them. And for both, the resurrection after almost 1700 years was to be the same.

The only thing that had survived the appalling tragedy was the precise, on the spot, account of Pliny the Younger, who even though he lost his uncle in the catastrophe, diligently, reported the details of that dramatic summer day in A.D. 79. The accuracy, the wealth of details, the precision of his account have without doubt been of great aid to archaeologists and scholars.

Pliny observed and described a terrible natural phenomenon, while thousands of persons died buried under a blanket of lava, ashes and lapilli and "many raised their hands to the gods, but almost all were convinced that the gods were there no longer."

The man who rediscovered Pompeii and Herculaneum in the 18th century did more than just bring to light two buried cities: he tied together, as if by magic, a broken thread, once more took up a discourse that had been cut short, in other words he gave life back to all those whom the gods had deprived of life.

HERCULANEUM

Herculaneum was situated on a promontory along the coast, between two rivers, and was on the main coastal thoroughfare which connected Neapolis to the towns of the gulf: Several ancient authors like Theophrastus, Sisenna, Dionysius of Halicarnassus, and Strabo mention Herculaneum in their works. Dyonisius says the town was founded by Hercules on his way back from Iberia; in this case the city would appear to have Greek origins. Strabo records it was under the domain of the Oscans, Tyrrhenians and Pelasgians and finally of the Samnites. Towards the end of the 4th century B. C. it was greatly influenced by the Greek town of Cuma and by Neapolis; it fell under the domain of the Samnites at the end of the 5th century B. C., like most cities of this region. In the period of the Social War it fought against Rome and in 89 B. C. was conquered by the legate of Silla, Titus Didius and became a Roman municipium. It soon became a holiday resort for many Roman patrician families, partly because of the beauty of the natural setting and partly because of its brilliant cultural life, largely influenced by Neapolis.

Herculaneum did not base its economic life on agriculture or on commerce, like Pompeii. All the same the style of life was very refined as we can assume by the many paintings which decorate the interior of most buildings and by the large number of statues which have been excavated. In 62 A.D. it was heavily damaged by an earthquake and in 79 A.D. it was buried by a mud avalanche, which has now hardened into tufa rock, and formed a stratum of about 12-18 metres of rocky lava. This explains the difficulties encountered by the excavators (Pompeii was covered by ash and lapilla) but at the same time explains why all the waste material, wooden furnishings and food which have proved very useful to scholars and for which Herculaneum is unique, have been preserved in good condition.

An aerial view of the city.

*Capo di Sorrento, a view of the so-called Queen
Joan's Bath* (Bagno della regina Giovanna).

SORRENTO

Set on the peninsula from which it takes its name, Sorrento is worthy of mention in its own right. It is a town of just under 18.000 inhabitants stretching out on a vulcanic tufa terrace which plunges down to the coast from high cliffs. The charm and natural beauty of this spot, exalted by the fertile citrus plantations, by the vast panorama over the gulf of Naples, Vesuvius and the Flegrean Fields and Islands, the extraordinarily transparent sea and the intensely clear blue sky, combine to make this town one of the sanctuaries of international tourism. An excellent hotel infrastructure, the remarkable quality of the services offered, and the wide variety of sports, recreation and cultural proposals on hand all go to make this a particularly attractive place to visit.

Although the origins of the name of this town are wrapped in mythology and the legend of the sirens *(Surrentum)*, it is a certain fact that the place was chosen by man as far back as the Neolithic age. It was probably colonized by the Greeks, followed by Etruscans, Siracusans and Samnites, before being occupied by the Romans who however were not willingly accepted by its inhabitants, who were constantly on the verge of rebellion. During the Imperial era the Roman patriarchs chose it as one of their favourite holiday places. After suffering Gothic and Byzantine occupations Sorrento managed to escape conquest by the Longobards but had to fight off the Saracenes and invaders from Amalfi. It was taken by the Normans in the first part of the 12th century and tried to overcome them with the help of the Republic of Pisa, but was finally brought into submission by King Roger. Sorely tried by internal contrast and by the struggles with its neighbours, Sorrento had a troubled history, made up of sieges and attempted conquests, up to the time of the founding of the Neapolitan Republic (end of the 18th century). The town was the birthplace of the famous 16th-century poet Torquato Tasso and became well-known as a residential area in the 18th century.

Ischia, impressive view of the Castle.

*From top: Capri, the Punta di Massullo with Curzio ▶
Malaparte's villa, the Faraglioni, the cliff of the Monacone
and the famous Grand Hotel Quisisana.*

THE ISLAND OF ISCHIA

The largest of the Parthenopean islands is, together with the nearby islands of Procida and Vivara, the result of an intense volcanic activity which overturned the Flegrean Fields region at the beginnings of geological history. The volcanic nature of the island, rather than the structure of its rocks (lava, tufa, magma of trachyte origin) can be deduced by the numerous craters (Montagnone, Mount Rotaro) and by the presence of an ancient volcano (Mount Epomeo), from the volcanic cauldron (the basin forming the port of Ischia) and from the intense thermal activity which together with the smoke-holes testify to a secondary volcanism which is still active.

The island was colonised in the 7th century B.C. by the Greeks who called it *Phitecusa* and was subsequently inhabited by people from Siracusa and then by the Romans who surrendered it to the Neapolitans in exchange for Capri in the 1st century A.D. It was renamed *Ischia* in the 9th century and came under the Angevins and Aragonese. After suffering repeated Saracene raids during the 16th and 17th centuries it passed to the Bourbons and took part in the national unification of 1861. The island has undergone frequent natural turmoils during its millennial history; from the eruptions which forced the Siracusans to flee (6th to 5th centuries B.C.), to that of 1302, including the ruinous earthquakes which have so often tried the tenacity and willpower of its population. The tremor which completely destroyed the village of Casamicciola on the 28th of July 1883 is tragically famous.

Ischia has been rightly named the "Emerald Island" because of its naturally lush Mediterranean vegetation and for the presence of plants which are more usually found in warmer climates.

THE ISLAND OF CAPRI

The geological structure of Capri is prevalently calcarea with the presence of tufa and pozzolana. The coasts, high and rocky, offer a large number of grottoes and are surrounded by rocks which rise out of the water, such as the *Faraglioni*. Of the many versions given for the origin of the place-name - *Caprea* according to Strabone, to indicate the harsh conformation of its soil, or *Capraim* which comes from the semitic expression "two villages" - *Capreae* is the more convincing because it would refer as Varrone ascertains, to the considerable presence of boars on the island (*Caprios* according to Greek spelling). The Roman "discovery" of Capri dates back to 29 B.C. when Augustus landed here on his way back after the Eastern campaigns. After the death of Augustus (14 A.D.) his successor Tiberius made Capri his "golden exile", choosing it as his home for the last decade of his life. His death (37 A.D.) marked the beginning of the decline. At the fall of the Roman Empire Capri was controlled by the abbots of Montecassino and by Neapolitans, and was subjected to pirate raids - especially those of the Saracens. Then it was controlled by the Longobards and by the Normans; the island passed from one domination to another including the Aragonese, Angevins, and the raids of the Turkish pirates Kahir ad-Din (Barbarossa) and Dragut. Then it came under Spanish administration and suffered a great plague (18th century), and then finally it was governed by the Bourbons. It was contended by the French and English at the time of the Napoleonic Wars, after which it was ruled once more by the Bourbons of Naples before its annexation to the newly formed Kingdom of Italy thereby establishing the characteristics which it now maintains as one of the obligatory stages of international tourism.